EZRA POUND

PETER ACKROYD

EZRA POUND

with 111 illustrations

THAMES AND HUDSON

ACKNOWLEDGMENTS

The author would like to thank Faber and Faber Ltd, and New Directions, New York, for permission to quote from Ezra Pound's works. Acknowledgments are due to Faber and Faber Ltd for: *ABC of Reading* 1951; *The Cantos of Ezra Pound* 1954, 3rd edition 1975; *The Classic Anthology Defined by Confucius* 1955; *Collected Early Poems of Ezra Pound* ed. Michael John King (incl. *A Lume Spento*) 1977; *Collected Shorter Poems* (incl. *Personae, Ripostes, Lustra*) 1952, 2nd edition 1968; *Selected Poems 1908–1959*, 1975; *Literary Essays of Ezra Pound* ed. T. S. Eliot 1954. For any material not included in the above editions, acknowledgment is due to the Ezra Pound Literary Property Trust and Faber and Faber Ltd. The following works are reprinted by permission of New Directions, New York: *A Lume Spento* Copyright © 1965 by Ezra Pound. All Rights Reserved. *Personae* (incl. *Cathay, Lustra, Ripostes, Hugh Selwyn Mauberley*) Copyright 1926 by Ezra Pound. *Women of Trachis* Copyright © 1957 by Ezra Pound. *Cantos* Copyright 1934, 1937, 1940, 1948, 1956, © 1959, 1962, 1963, 1968, 1969, 1972 by The Trustees of the Ezra Pound Literary Property Trust. *ABC of Reading* Copyright 1934 by Ezra Pound. *Selected Letters* (1907–1941) Copyright 1950 by Ezra Pound. *Gaudier-Brzeska* Copyright © 1970 by Ezra Pound. All Rights Reserved. *Guide to Kulchur* Copyright © 1970 by Ezra Pound. All Rights Reserved. *Selected Prose 1909–1965* Copyright © 1973 by The Trustees of the Ezra Pound Literary Property Trust. All Rights Reserved. *Make It New* Copyright 1935, © 1963 by Ezra Pound. *Ezra Pound and Music* ed. R. Murray Schafer (*Antheil and the Treatise on Harmony*) Copyright © 1977 by The Trustees of the Ezra Pound Literary Property Trust. All Rights Reserved. Quotations from essays published in small magazines, with details about publications, are also reprinted by permission of New Directions, New York. *The Classic Anthology*, here entitled *Confucian Odes*, is published by Harvard University Press. Copyright 1954 by the President and Fellows of Harvard College. *Jefferson and/or Mussolini* is published in the USA by Liveright. Copyright 1935, 1936 by Ezra Pound.

THE FIRST NOTE is a characteristic one. Strawberries were dangled on a string 'to teach the infant Gargantua to look about; to look "up" and to be ready for the benefits of the gods, whether so whither they might come upon him.' The 'infant Gargantua' here is Ezra Pound's description of himself in *Indiscretions*, an autobiographical sketch, and the poet's capacity for myth-making – even about his earliest infancy – was never to desert him. The place in which he was born, however, encouraged such fantasies since it had very little to offer in their place: Hailey, Idaho, was a 'frontier town'; the first building had been constructed in 1810 and, by the time Ezra Pound was born, on 30 October 1885, it boasted just one street which contained, according to Pound, forty-seven saloons and one hotel.

But although Pound was continually to revert to his origins in this folksy Midwest, his family actually moved to Philadelphia in 1889 and finally settled in Wyncote, a small town nearby, when Pound was seven. This move away from his 'roots' seems to have affected him deeply – in retrospect at least; both in his life and his work he tried to reconstruct the mythical America from which he imagined he had come. He wrote to Thomas Hardy in 1921, 'I come from an American suburb – where I was not born – where both parents are really

Pound was born here on 30 October 1885 and it was his home for the first eighteen months of his life. The first plastered house in the 'frontier town' of Hailey, Idaho, it was built by his father, Homer.

A modern photograph of Pound's home at 166 Fernbrook Avenue, Wyncote, Pennsylvania. He was to live here intermittently, from the age of six to twenty-two, until he left for Europe.

foreigners.' And the year before, he had written (in *The New Age*), 'I was brought up in a city with which my forebears had no connection and I am therefore accustomed to being alien in one place or another.'

Since the infant Pound had moved only as far as Pennsylvania, this notion of being 'alien' may seem a somewhat exaggerated one (in fact, Pound's comments about himself and his work have always to be treated with a certain suspicion), especially since he was granted all the comforts and familial adoration which an only child can often elicit. Pound's father, Homer, held the post of assistant assayer at the United States Mint; this was appropriate employment in the light of his son's later economic obsessions, and Ezra Pound was to recall one visit with his father to 'the Mint vaults, the bags had rotted, and the men half-naked with open gas flares, shovelled [the coins] into the

counting-machines, with a gleam on tarnished discs'. Homer Pound himself was a genial and affectionate man, who remained continually and genuinely astonished by his son's prowess as a writer and as a poet. 'There isn't a darn thing that boy of mine don't know,' he was to tell Max Beerbohm in the Thirties. Ezra Pound's mother, Isabel, was rather more aloof and suffered from a slight excess of gentility – interested in 'culture', albeit of a conventional kind, and deeply ambitious for her son.

Both parents were 'Yankees' of the old-fashioned sort, being both shrewd and individualistic – the race before the flood of European immigrants who were to transform American life in the new century. Homer Pound's father, Thaddeus, had in fact been born in a log cabin but – in conventional Midwestern fashion – started a prosperous lumbering business (where he issued his own private currency) and

Wyncote, *c.* 1893. Pound was to say later of this town, 'The suburb has no roots, no center of life.' On his release from St Elizabeth's in 1958 Pound returned here and walked the streets alone.

Wyncote Public School, in Greenwood Avenue, the 'official school' attended by Pound from June 1895 to June 1897. It turned out to be a rather stricter establishment than any he had attended before.

eventually became a Congressman. In this sense Ezra Pound's later populism was indigenous to the familial soil in which he grew, a populism both quirky and radical, and one which could be easily lured toward racism. 'But I (der grosse Ich)', Pound wrote to the poet William Carlos Williams in 1917, 'have the virus, the bacillus of the land in my blood, for nearly three bleating centuries.' It is only a short step from this blood tie to Pound's later and virulent anti-Semitism. And when Pound broadcast from Rome in 1942, 'This is my war all right. I have been in it for twenty years – my grand-dad was in it before me,' the derivations become clear.

At the time, of course, such matters hardly impinged upon the Pound family. Although Pound was to comment disparagingly on 'the encroachment of one personality upon another in the sty of the family', there seems to have been remarkably little tension in the household. He was known as 'Ra' or 'Ray'; he was spoiled a little and, although there is no external evidence of any marked precocity, 'Ra' himself seems to have fixed upon his destiny very early in life. He wrote in an article, 'How I Began', 'I knew at fifteen pretty much what I wanted to do. I believed that the "impulse" is with the gods;

that technique is a man's own responsibility. I resolved that at thirty I would know more about poetry than any man living.' The atmosphere in which he formed this resolve was not, perhaps, conducive to the highest achievement; contemporary American verse was neither interesting nor significant, and the standard poetry appeared in volumes like *Poems for Travellers, Birds of the Poets* and *Poets on Christmas*. Pound was to say, in an interview many years later, 'The impression then was that the American stuff wasn't quite as good as the English at any point.'

But Pound set out, with characteristic determination, to educate himself; he was enrolled, when in his own words 'a lanky whey-faced youth', at the University of Pennsylvania in Philadelphia in 1901. Here he was soon reading Catullus, Browning and Ernest Dowson – significant influences on his own later poetry. He seems at first to have been reserved and untalkative, noticeable to his contemporaries at college only for his hard and assiduous study. He was in many ways a model pupil, with a pronounced interest in the kind of sustained book-reading that was to breed in him subsequently both the virtues and the vices of the pedagogue.

The chorus in Euripides' *Iphigenia among the Taurians*, undergraduates at the University of Pennsylvania, April 1903. William Carlos Williams wrote that Pound (second from left in this photograph) 'waved his arms about and heaved his massive breasts in ecstasies of extreme emotion'.

At the University of Pennsylvania, Pound met a fellow student who was to play an important role in his erratic career – William Carlos Williams. They were introduced through a mutual friend in 1902, and Williams was immediately impressed by Pound's intellectual precocity and apparent self-confidence. He wrote in his *Autobiography*, 'Ezra never explained or joked about his writing . . . He joked, crudely, about anything but that. I was fascinated by the man. He was the livest, most intelligent and unexplainable thing that I'd ever seen, and the most fun – except for his often painful self-consciousness and his coughing laugh.' They rapidly became close friends and remained so although, like all Pound's friendships, it was more often honoured in spirit than in observance. Pound could, according to Williams, be 'warm and devoted', but he could also be bitchy and peremptory. Despite all his manifest charm and showmanship, there was a cold and impersonal element within his temperament: 'One trait I always held against Ezra', Williams wrote, 'was that he'd never let you in on his personal affairs.' It was a trait that was to become more pronounced with the years.

In 1903 Pound left Pennsylvania to study at Hamilton College at Clinton in New York State; here he rapidly became a 'character' and, again according to Williams, 'was the laughing stock of the place'. He was restless, self-conscious, nervous, constantly talking. But his manner, in fact, only became remarkable when his sense of his own

Left: William Carlos Williams, the American poet who became a close friend of Pound's at the University of Pennsylvania. Williams described Pound during this period as 'vicious, catty at times, neglectful if he trusted you not to mind, but warm and devoted'.

Right: The chess team, from the *Hamiltonian*, 1905. Pound looks more relaxed than usual; a description of him at this time states that 'he rushed along with a long stride. Constantly talking.'

Below: A picture of Pound, from the *Hamiltonian*, 1906. 'Peroxide blonde' he may have been, but during this period he was also composing some of the poetry which was to appear in his first volume, *A Lume Spento*.

Ezra Weston Pound,   Philadelphia, Pa.

"Ezra"

"Bib's" pride.   Leader of the anvil chorus at the Commons.   Oh, how he throws those legs! Peroxide blonde.

powers had grown more pronounced: his studies were consciously directed toward the high literary goals which he had set for himself, and at Hamilton he read widely in Anglo-Saxon, in the Romance languages, and in medieval history. This combination proved a potent one, since it became the cultural and historical field in which he wandered for the rest of his life.

Pound claimed, much later, that he had always been dissatisfied with the nature of academic life in the United States during this period: 'In my university', he wrote in *How To Read*, 'I found various men interested (or uninterested) in their subjects, but, I think, no man with a view of literature as a whole.' There seems little reason to doubt, however, that at this stage he was an assiduous and ambitious student preparing himself for a 'career'. At all events, he returned to the University of Pennsylvania in 1905 for further study, and became a Master of Arts in June of the following year.

But it was also during this period that Pound began what was to become his most significant work. He said, in an interview in the *Paris Review*, 'I began the *Cantos* about 1904, I suppose.' And, although there is no record of any work done at that time which emerged in the published *Cantos*, he was indeed already obsessed with the epic tone. By 1904 he possessed a copy of Spenser's *The Faerie Queene* and the 1713 edition of Milton's *Paradise Lost*. The idea of the long poem, the 'epic including history', was one that came early and stayed until the end.

The work of a young poet is often dissipated by self-conscious 'ideas', or by the pressure of imitation and romantic improvisation; but Ezra Pound's poetry is distinctive from the beginning because of its formal clarity and its technical discipline. He worked hard to improve his craft – not only to know more about poetry than any man living, but also to explore the possibilities of each poetic form. Williams comments that, at the University of Pennsylvania, Pound was 'writing a daily sonnet. He destroyed them all at the end of the year.' Pound impressed other contemporaries also. Hilda Doolittle (better known as the poet 'H.D.') was a student at Bryn Mawr, and their meeting in 1905 led to an unofficial 'engagement'. She described Pound as 'immensely sophisticated, immensely superior, immensely rough-and-ready . . . One would dance with him for what he might say.' He introduced her to the work of Ibsen, Shaw, Morris, Blake, and even Swedenborg – a testament to his polymathy, if not his judgment.

In 1906 Pound became a Harrison Fellow in Romantics at the University of Pennsylvania, and continued the familiar routine of post-graduate work there. His research was mainly concerned with the Provençal poets and the plays of Lope de Vega, two projects which gave him the opportunity to revisit the one area which haunted his imagination – Europe. He had travelled there twice before with various members of his family, but it was the idea of a literary, quasi-medieval Europe which exercised the most powerful attraction. Indeed it could have remained simply a learned and imagined terrain

Opposite: Hilda Doolittle, better known as the poet 'H.D.' Pound met her in 1905, and they became unofficially engaged. Between 1905 and 1907 he wrote *Hilda's Book*, a collection of poems showing early signs of promise.

if Pound had continued on his academic treadmill. But circumstances were soon to force him off this, and into the 'real world'.

On his return from Europe, Pound took up an academic post at Wabash College in Crawfordsville, Indiana. It was the autumn of 1907, and from the beginning he began to languish. Even the intermittently interesting milieu of Pennsylvania was missing here – as he wrote in a poem at that time,

> And I am homesick
> After my own kind . . .

Whatever his 'kind' might be, it was certainly not to be found in a small-town American college; and Pound's rumbling dislike for the constraints of academic life surfaced in one incident which changed the entire course of his early career. In a characteristically charitable gesture – so it is assumed – Pound shared a meal in his Wabash rooms with a young actress. Certain accounts suggest that she stayed the night, while Pound slept elsewhere. At all events the lady was discovered within his walls, and Pound was asked to leave Wabash College.

This incident is frequently recalled in Pound's correspondence. He had by no means courted this rejection, and it must have come as something of a shock. From then on, he never ceased to attack the American academic system. He abandoned any attempt at a conventional career, and took on instead the role of the 'outsider'. He had often in the past posed as a rebel while actually enjoying the fruits of the system against which he was ostensibly rebelling; but now a real decision was forced upon him. Hilda Doolittle wrote in her memoir, *End to Torment*, 'Almost everyone I knew in Philadelphia was against him, after that Wabash College debacle.' Pound himself was not immune to gossip: 'They say', he told her, 'that I am bisexual and given to unnatural lust.' And so Pound left Wabash and travelled back to that place which, from the beginning, had seemed to offer an alternative life: Europe. He was to spend most of the next forty years there. In October 1907 he wrote to Viola Baxter, a girl whom he had met in New York State, 'Poetry is my "metier", the only one of the arts in which I have progressed beyond the kindergarten stages. Anything I do outside it is a make-shift, a contrivance to preserve.' And now he had the chance to prove it.

In February 1908 he sailed across the Atlantic and, through some intuitive sense of place, arrived in late spring in Venice – the city which, more than any other, was to be implicated in his strange destiny. At first he lived above a bakery, and then in San Trovaso – opposite a gondola repair shop. It was a time of indecision and indigence (he had arrived in Italy with only eighty dollars). His new role was that of the expatriate poet, but he hadn't yet found an appropriate stage. And his voice was still an uncertain one – despite the fact that, in June of 1908, he paid the sum of eight dollars to have his first volume of poems printed.

It was entitled *A Lume Spento* (With Tapers Quenched). Its overall tone is in many ways a conventionally elegiac one, but the strength of line and variety of form suggest the presence of a talent harder and deeper than the surface content of the poems themselves:

> I have sung women in three cities
> But it is all one.
>
> I will sing of the white birds
> In the blue waters of heaven,
> The clouds that are spray to its sea.

These lines are from 'Cino', an Italian poet and jurist, who is here supposed to be speaking. Pound's use of this persona is characteristic of his early poetry; his sense of his own identity was as yet obscure or unformulated – '(I? I? I? I?)', he wrote in the same volume of poems – and he tended to play instead with a series of masks and dramatic voices. But even at this stage, Pound was instinctively aware of the central poetic role he was about to assume. His rejection by Wabash was only the first of a series of rejections which he was later

The gondola repair shop opposite Pound's room in the San Trovaso quarter of Venice, *c.* 1908. This was one of the happiest periods of Pound's life, and he was to recall it in his later work:

And the waters richer than glass,
Bronze gold, the blaze over the silver,
Dye-pots in the torch light,
The flash of waves under prows.

(Canto XVII)

15

A
LUME
SPENTO

EZRA POUND.

This Book was

LA FRAISNE

(THE ASH TREE)

dedicated

*to such as love this same
beauty that I love, somewhat
after mine own fashion.*

But sith one of them has gone out very quickly from
amongst us it given

A LUME SPENTO

(WITH TAPERS QUENCHED)

in memoriam eius mihi caritate primus

William Brooke Smith

Painter, Dreamer of dreams.

A Lume Spento, printed in a first edition of only 100 copies in June 1908. Pound had doubts about the collection, and was about to consign it to the waters of Venice, but fortunately he relented. His career as poet and self-propagandist had begun. He wrote to his parents: 'The American reprint has got to be worked by kicking up such a hell of a row with genuine and faked reviews. I shall write a few myself and get someone to sign 'em.' *Left:* Title page and *right:* dedication from the first edition. William Brooke Smith, a painter whom Pound had met in Philadelphia, was 'my first friend'.

consciously to draw upon himself; and the poems he wrote during this period are delivered, in the main, through the voice of 'le poète maudit'. He wrote to William Carlos Williams at this time, 'If you mean to say that *A Lume Spento* is a rather gloomy and disagreeable book, I agree with you . . . Then again you must remember that I don't try to write for the public. I can't. I haven't that kind of intelligence.'

This turned out to be more accurate a diagnosis than he could possibly know. In the *Cantos*, he returns to the young man he once was in Venice with a sense of loss and regret:

> And at night they sang in the gondolas
> And in the barche with lanthorns;
> The prows rose silver on silver
>   taking light in the darkness.

Then, everything had been before him. And in *A Lume Spento* he had staked his claim:

> *Manus animam pinxit—*
> My pen is in my hand.

Pound, *c.* 1908–10. One of the first photographs taken of him after he had moved to London; note the actorish pose. Brigit Patmore has described this aspect of his character: 'He was at ease in masquerade, without being self-conscious or acting. It helped him, I think, to keep inviolable.'

Pen in hand, Pound travelled to London in September 1908. 'Want to have a month up the Thames somewhere and meet Bill Yeats', he wrote to William Carlos Williams. 'Up the Thames' is a little vague, but such brashness would not go unrewarded.

Pound's descriptions of the cultural and social life of London were not always flattering: 'When I arrived in England (AD 1908) I found a greater darkness in the British "serious press" than had obtained on the banks of the Schuylkill,' he wrote in *How To Read*. And, later, in *Jefferson And/Or Mussolini*: 'London stank of decay before 1914 . . . London was in terror of thought.' But these are all comments after the event – after Pound felt himself to have been rejected by the 'serious press' and everyone else in the malignant city. At the time, on his arrival from Venice, he was more sanguine about the place: 'London, deah old Lundon, is the place for poesy.' Even five years later, when part of the 'deah' bloom had worn off, he was writing, 'London is a great picture book, and its pages of infinite variety.'

Indeed at first Pound had some cause to be grateful to London, and for those habits of thought and behaviour which he was later to revile.

Thomas E. Hulme, *c.* 1914. Hulme, the English philosopher and poet, befriended Pound and introduced him to the purlieus of literary London.

When he arrived from Italy, carrying with him a few copies of *A Lume Spento*, he knew practically no one. But, after only a modicum of effort on his part, he was 'taken up'. He was published, he was read, he was something of a success. The conditions were, in a sense, appropriate. Although the literary dispensation of the time was stolid and somewhat unconvincing – with Bennett, Shaw, Belloc and Chesterton huffing and puffing in the foreground ('All degrading the values,' as Pound was to write later) – the prevailing cultural atmosphere was not as moribund as Pound was inclined, in retrospect, to think. Fashionable European movements – Symbolism, Impressionism, Post-Impressionism – were appreciated if not entirely understood, and London was still a centre of literary activity. Pound could quite happily hawk his poems around Fleet Street, in the hope that they would be published by the national press, and the popular dailies paid an inordinate amount of attention to the more scandalous aspects of modernist art and literature. Publishers were happy to produce books with short print runs and only a limited expectation of life, and there was an enormous variety of literary magazines. It was in fact possible, as Pound discovered, to earn a modest income simply by writing for such journals – an unthinkable prospect today.

The atmosphere of London, then, was not entirely uncongenial to Pound, and within a few weeks he had left his visiting card – in the form of some copies of *A Lume Spento*, which he deposited at the bookshop of Elkin Mathews. Mr Mathews was also a publisher and, on the strength of a handful of good reviews of Pound's book (Pound was always adept, albeit in a circumspect way, at publicizing his own work), he decided to publish a further collection, *Personae*. Pound has conveyed what is no doubt an accurate description of the mechanics of the business:

Mr E. M. 'Ah, eh, do you care to contribute to the costs of publishing?'
Mr E. P. 'I've got a shilling in my clothes, if that's any use to you.'
Mr E. M. 'Oh well, I rather want to publish 'em anyhow.'

Although Pound did only possess a shilling or two – he scraped together a little money by lecturing – he was quickly learning how to meet and influence people. Through Mathews he came across T. E. Hulme, a poet and theorist who exercised far more influence than his shadowy reputation now suggests. It has been said, in fact, that Hulme's theory of the image and his notions of a 'pure' language profoundly affected the course of Pound's early poetic development – although this seems to me to be improbable. Despite his earnest desire to be, and to be seen as, 'the poet', his literary convictions at this stage were too diffuse to be affected significantly by any one person or programme. In any event, his aspirations in London were still predominantly social ones. He met interesting or, at least, important people like the poet and translator, Laurence Binyon, and the actress, Ellen Terry. He was taken to the Poet's Club and the Square Club, two of the more solid literary fraternities of the metropolis. In fact Pound could easily have become an Edwardian among the Edwardians – if he had not been both more gifted and more eccentric than other aspiring writers of that period.

Pound was fortunate, too, in his friendships. In these first years he met Olivia Shakespear and her daughter, Dorothy, who was to become his wife in 1914. Dorothy recorded her early impressions in an understandably sentimental way: 'He has a wonderful, beautiful face, a high forehead, prominent over the eyes, a long, delicate nose . . . you are all a dream – all your ideas, your knowledge, your bluey eyes; all your great loneliness.' But it was in 1909 that he met two people who were to exercise a more immediate influence upon his life: Ford Madox Ford (then known as Ford Madox Hueffer) and W. B. Yeats. Pound had already expressed the wish to 'meet Bill Yeats' and, after a certain amount of effort, he was successful. They were introduced by the Shakespears, and Yeats immediately took to the younger man. By the middle of 1909 Pound was attending Yeats's 'Monday evenings', and very soon he had taken them over. Douglas Goldring has described the scene in a memoir of the period, *South Lodge*: 'He

Olivia Shakespear, Dorothy's mother, and one of Pound's first friends in London. She was, he wrote to his parents, 'undoubtedly the most charming woman in London'.

dominated the room, distributed Yeats's cigarettes and Chianti, and laid down the law about poetry.' Yeats forgave him this, and everything else; there was a peculiar empathy between the two poets which survived the manifest differences in their age and their poetry – although perhaps in temperament (hardness, masked by flights of self-dramatizing fancy) they were alike.

Ford, too, was to prove useful. He had recently begun to edit *The English Review*, an ambitious and perspicacious journal which had already published the work of Joseph Conrad, Thomas Hardy and Henry James. It was soon to give space to D. H. Lawrence, Wyndham Lewis and Pound himself. In *Return to Yesterday*, Ford has described how Pound came upon the scene: 'Ezra would approach with the steps of a dancer, making passes with a cane at an imaginary opponent. He would wear trousers made of green billiard cloth, a pink coat, a blue shirt, a tie hand-painted by a Japanese friend, an immense sombrero, a flaming beard cut to a point and a single, large blue ear-ring.' Pound's flamboyant appearance may at first have been enough to interest Ford, who was a connoisseur of eccentricity. He

⁂ THE
ENGLISH
REVIEW

APRIL 1910

LONDON : CHAPMAN & HALL LTD.
PUBLISHED MONTHLY 2/6 NET

Ford Madox Ford (previously known as Ford Madox Hueffer). 'I made my life in London', Pound was to say many years later, 'by going to see Ford in the afternoons and Yeats in the evenings.'

'took up' the young American poet and published his 'Sestina: Altaforte' in *The English Review* of June 1909.

Pound was at least a step on his way and, according to Ford, it was a rapid journey: 'In a very short time he had taken charge of me, the review and finally of London.' Pound's proprietorial air toward Ford is very much like that which he adopted toward Yeats – as though Pound had always, in a sense, to be 'in charge'. Pound himself, of course, saw such matters in rather grander terms: 'The revolution of the word began,' he wrote later in *Polite Essays*, 'so far as it affected the men who were of my age in London in 1908, with the LONE whimper of Ford Madox Hueffer.' The peevish note of 'whimper' here is not altogether satisfactory, and Pound put his point better in an interview which he gave towards the end of his life: 'One was hunting for a simple and natural language and Ford was ten years older, and accelerated the process towards it . . . Ford knew the best of the people who were there before him, you see, and he had nobody to play with until Wyndham and I and my generation came along.' Ford's

Opposite: Cover of the *English Review*, 1910, the formidable periodical edited by Ford Madox Ford. A glance at the contents shows the range and perspicacity of Ford's interests; he was the first editor to publish Pound's poetry in England.

10 Church Walk, Kensington. Pound lived here, with short breaks, from 1909 to 1914. He wrote later to a biographer, 'You can make Kens the center of my activity, with forays into quite other atmospheres.'

friendship and advice were invaluable; it was, Pound said many years later to the American poet, Charles Olson, 'the high period of my life'.

The 'Wyndham' whom Pound mentions is Wyndham Lewis. When they first met in 1909 they were wary of each other: 'Ezra was an uncomfortably tensed, nervously straining, jerky, reddish-brown young American,' Lewis wrote. But he was able accurately to gauge the actual effect of Pound upon the English: 'He was like a drop of oil in a glass of water; the trouble was, I believe, that he had no wish to *mix*: he just wanted to *impress* . . .' D. H. Lawrence, who met Pound in the same year, at first thought him 'a good bit of a genius, and with not the least self-consciousness', but soon found him too oppressively theatrical, and by 1910 was describing him as a 'sort of latest edition of *jongleur*'.

Although Pound was indeed nervous and self-conscious during these years, saying the first thing that came into his head, he had not yet become the prickly rebel, the virulently anti-establishment man in all things. His appearance and behaviour were unsettling or amusing, according to taste – he ate rose petals at Ernest Rhys's dinner table, on one occasion – but he did not as yet pose a serious threat to the Edwardian dispensation. He seems, in fact, to have adapted to it with a certain amount of ease; he had moved to a pleasant room in Church Walk, Kensington, his poems were being published in English periodicals, and, in 1909, he published two books of poetry – *Personae* and *Exultations* – which achieved a measure of critical success. In other words, he was still keeping his options open; he was not entirely estranged from the old world of Edwardian letters, but he was spending more and more time with those men – Ford, Lewis, Hulme – who were challenging the literary conventions of the time.

Pound, however, did not play any significant part in their activities: he was not yet wholly enamoured of radical change, simply because he wasn't sure of his own mind in such matters. The influence of Ford had already suggested to him that a 'revolution of the word' was both necessary and important but, as he put it in *Make It New*, 'I hadn't in 1910 made a language. I don't mean a language to use, but even a language to think in.' His own work of the period bears some of the marks of this ambiguity. The poems in the two collections of 1909 are confidently handled, with a mastery of form and technique which is so assured that sometimes they move close to parody, but the voice is hesitant and troubled. The tone of the poetry hovers somewhere between aesthetic withdrawal into the conventions of Pre-Raphaelite lyric and a more robust, though equally derivative, 'heroic' manner. Occasionally, however, the beginnings of a coherent voice emerge:

> I who have seen you amid the primal things
> Was angry when they spoke your name
> In ordinary places . . .

It ought to be said in fairness, though, that Pound put this creative hesitancy in a more deliberate and determined perspective. He wrote,

Wyndham Lewis, a portrait by Augustus John. Pound and Lewis first met in 1909 when, according to Pound in the *Cantos*, they behaved like two wary bulldogs. Pound, according to Lewis, was 'a charitable egoist'.

in an essay in 1914, 'I began this search for the real in a book called *Personae*, casting off, as it were, complete masks of the self in each poem. I continued in a long series of translations, which were but more elaborate masks.' This notion of 'mask', whether through the medium of translation or the adopted persona, was important to Pound because, as we have seen, he still had no real sense of his own language or of his proper self; and so he took refuge in the surfaces of his personality and of his words – in his role-playing for the Londoners, and in his mastery of delicate and improbable poetic forms.

In *The Spirit of Romance*, Pound's first book of prose criticism (published in 1910 but adapted from lectures of 1908 and 1909), the writer's self-confidence and broad scholarship are, paradoxically, a result of this absence of finely honed self-knowlege. The study is still

25

worth serious consideration. It covers a great deal of ground, moving from Dante to Villon and the Provençal poet, Arnaut Daniel, and is bright and bracing, with a number of swift and unerring critical judgments which are all the more forceful for their eschewal of academic jargon. (It is ironic, incidentally, that the poet who has become a central point of academic study should himself have been so resolutely anti-academic.) And despite occasional naivety and frequent dashes into unproven assertion, the intelligence and the spirit of Pound's mature criticism are already in evidence: 'Poetry is about as much a "criticism of life" as red-hot iron is a criticism of fire.'

In 1910 Pound travelled to France, Italy, and then on to the United States, where he stayed for some months. Rather in the mood of the returning hero, he made good use of his time. While there, for example, he met John Quinn, a lawyer and patron of the arts, and realized that Quinn's generous enthusiasm might prove helpful in a variety of ways. The good diviner knows by intuition where the gold is to be found; Pound knew, and he dug. His entrepreneurial gifts came early and, even in the worst of times, never deserted him. Over the next few years, Quinn was to become Pound's unofficial agent, confidant, secretary and – on other people's behalf – bank.

Pound returned to England in February 1911, but he was off again almost immediately – to Europe, and this time with Yeats. Such restlessness was a marked characteristic of Pound during this period of uncertainty. He was always in flight – whether from himself, in masks and personae, or from those people and places that had helped to nourish him. Eliot, who was to meet Pound a few years later, characterized the manner very well:

. . . He seemed always to be a temporary squatter. The appearance was due not only to his restless energy – in which it was difficult to distinguish the energy from the restlessness and the fidgets, so that every room, even a big one, seemed too small for him – but to a kind of resistance against growing into any environment. In America he would no doubt have always seemed on the point of going abroad; in London, he always seemed on the point of crossing the Channel.

But when Pound did eventually return to England, in the summer of 1911, he was, if not more composed, at least more certain of himself. Although *Canzoni*, a volume of conventionally archaic poems – the ornate diction of which had caused Ford Madox Ford to roll on the floor in paroxysms of embarrassment and glee – had been published earlier that year, Pound was now forming a more substantial idea of his own work and of his possible future as a writer. It was fortunate, also, that these new perceptions found a ready-made vehicle for their expression: through Hulme, Pound met A. R. Orage who was the editor of the radical journal, *The New Age*. By the end of 1911, Pound was putting forward a critical philosophy in its pages which, for him at least, was entirely new. In a sequence of articles, entitled 'I Gather The Limbs of Osiris', Pound laid down the principles which were continually to affect his writing: 'As to twentieth century poetry, and the poetry I expect to see written during the next decade or so, it will, I think, move against poppy-cock; it will be harder and saner . . . At least for myself, I want it so, austere, direct, free from emotional slither.'

As always in Pound's writings, the critical ideas may not be entirely original but, once he had taken possession of them, he publicized them with gusto. As soon as he had grasped a theory, he wanted to put it directly into practice; ideas became manifestos, writers were transformed into cabals. It was doubly fortunate, then, that in 1912 he should have two friends to assist him with his new cause: Hilda Doolittle and Richard Aldington. Hilda Doolittle had recently arrived in London to visit her old but unofficial fiancé. Aldington had met Pound at the beginning of 1912 when the American was, in Aldington's words, 'a small but persistent volcano in the dim levels of London literary society. London was interested and amused by him. The evening papers interviewed him at length and published his portrait.' And now Pound was ready to make a bigger splash; the pool was prepared, and his diving board was 'Imagism'.

It all seems to have begun in a teashop. Pound had an inordinate fondness for pastry, and Aldington traced the origins of the new movement among one afternoon's buns and cakes: 'Ezra was so worked up by these poems of H.D.'s that he removed his pince-nez

The list of contents from *Des Imagistes*, a volume edited by Pound which was published in 1914. The edition sold out. As Richard Aldington, one of the contributors, wrote later: 'Evidently we were at least a succès de scandale.'

CONTENTS

5

6

and informed us we were Imagists.' Hilda Doolittle herself remembers Pound giving her literary advice in the tea-room of the British Museum: 'Cut this out,' he told her, 'shorten this line.' And then, in conclusion, he scratched the words 'H.D. Imagiste' at the bottom of her manuscript. In fact, once Pound had organized such things, they became faiths which required complete adherence. According to Aldington: 'Ezra was a bit of a czar in a small but irritating way.' And so, with the certainty of Pound's absolute faith in his own intuitions, Imagism was formed. It was to be 'hard and sane', and it was meant to be exclusive: 'Ezra would obliterate a literary figure by the simple constatation, "Il n'est pas dong le mouvemong."'

But 'le mouvemong' did have its more serious aspect, with its concerted attack upon the prevailing poetic diction of the period – an attack reinforced by Ford's 'revolution of the word', but also by Pound's growing mastery of his own language in the poetry he was now writing. The poetic demands which Imagism set were strict ones:

1. Direct treatment of the 'thing', whether subjective or objective.
2. To use absolutely no word that does not contribute to the presentation.
3. As regarding rhythm: to compose in the sequence of the musical phrase, not in sequence of a metronome.

At last Pound was making more than a personal impression; and, although the Imagist movement was not destined to survive for more than two years, it complemented the growing maturity of Pound's own writing. *Ripostes*, a volume published in 1912, is larger and longer than its predecessors – its physical presence emphasizing the increased seriousness of Pound's enterprise. The verse itself is more flexible, more direct; and, although much of the work is still derivative, in certain poems Pound is at last able to harness the demotic rhythms of speech to present directly his vision of the world. Such speech rhythms have now become a popular, indeed a conventional, poetic style, but at the time it was an important undertaking: to excise orthodox rhetoric and replace it with the natural rhythms of good prose:

> Great minds have sought you – lacking someone else.
> You have been second always. Tragical?
> No. You preferred it to the usual thing:
> One dull man, dulling and uxorious,
> One average mind – with one thought less, each year.

The title of the poem from which these lines are taken, 'Portrait d'une Femme', suggests the novelistic influences on Pound's new work. It was now his belief that good 'modern' poetry must take account of the context and the achievements of prose narrative – and then go further, and better, in the mode of vivid re-enactment. This was an unexpected and ambitious way of understanding the language of poetry; and it is hardly surprising that, with *Ripostes*, Ezra Pound lost some of his old audience, or that his work and reputation came increasingly under attack.

RIPOSTES
OF
EZRA POUND

WHERETO ARE APPENDED THE
COMPLETE POETICAL WORKS OF
T. E. HULME

WITH PREFATORY NOTE

LONDON
ELKIN MATHEWS, CORK STREET
MCMXV

His standing in London literary circles wasn't helped, either, by his first serious efforts to publicize and propagandize what he considered the best modern work. Harriet Monroe, the editor of *Poetry* magazine in Chicago, had written to Pound in August 1912, asking him to send her some of his work. A long correspondence followed, in the course of which Pound (sensing that in *Poetry* he had a vehicle of which he could take command) impressed upon Monroe the seriousness of her role: 'Can you teach the American poet that poetry *is* an *art*, an art with a technique, with media . . . I'm sick to loathing of people who don't care for the master-work.' In September Pound became foreign editor of *Poetry*, thus beginning a collaboration that was to bear strange and unexpected fruit. It was a fresh start, a turning point in Pound's life. As he was to write later, in *Make It New*, 'Let it stand that from 1912 onward for a decade and more I was instrumental in forcing into print, and *secondarily* in commenting on, certain work now recognized as valid by all competent readers.' Pound's connection with *Poetry* was the first step in a career during which, practically single-handed, he was to shape the public recognition and understanding of 'modern' poetry.

Ripostes, 1915 edition, originally published in 1912. Elkin Mathews agreed to republish the volume after the first publisher went into liquidation. Pound quotes Mathews as saying to him a year later 'Why, why will you needlessly irritate people?' *Left:* Cover, designed by Dorothy Shakespear. The quasi-Vorticist design suggests that she was much influenced by her husband's enthusiasms. *Right:* Title page.

The real missionary work began in 1913. He helped to publish and 'puff' the poetry of William Carlos Williams and Robert Frost – who was living in England at this time – although Frost himself was ungenerous: 'Pound is an incredible ass and hurts more than he helps the person he praises,' he wrote to a friend in October 1913. But Pound was never affected by other people's misgivings. He even endured the patronage, and later the hostility, of Amy Lowell in his struggles on behalf of Imagism. It was a busy time. He went to Paris in April, in order to spread the word, where John Gould Fletcher, an American poet, describes him as 'shielded by a pince-nez . . . a high-pitched, shrill almost feminine voice provided strange contrast to the pugnacious virility of the poet's general aspect . . . As baffling a bundle of contradictions as any man whom I had ever known.' On his return, Pound became literary editor of *The New Freewoman* (later to be known as *The Egoist*) where his burgeoning interests found another platform. A collection of short, epigrammatic poems, 'Contemporania', was published in *Poetry* during this year, and caused something of a stir because of their 'obscenity' and satirical directness. And Pound was also working on a volume of poems, *Lustra*, which was to be his most achieved and coherent to date.

Perhaps the most important event of 1913 was Pound's meeting in London with Henri Gaudier-Brzeska, a young sculptor whose alert perceptiveness and somewhat eccentric notions of cultural history were profoundly to affect Pound's awareness of modern art and sculpture. Brzeska was to die two years later, on a battlefield in France, but Pound recorded their brief friendship in a study of the sculptor's work: 'He was certainly the best company in the world, and some of my best days, the happiest and most interesting, were spent in his uncomfortable mud-floored studio when he was doing my bust.' The bust survived, and was to be carted all over Europe by Pound in the course of his later wanderings. It was a permanent reminder of a man, and a whole past, destroyed by the events of the world. Many years later, when Pound was incarcerated in an asylum, his psychiatric inquisitors were said to believe that Gaudier-Brzeska's death had materially affected Pound's sanity.

For the time being, however, everything seemed to be moving into place. Pound was at last certain of the direction in which he should go, and he had never been more active – often in the most unexpected ways. It was in this year, for example, that he came across the Fenollosa manuscripts. Ernest Fenollosa was an American scholar who had lived in Japan for many years. While there he had been working on the translation of Chinese and Japanese poetry but, on his death, he left his notes in a tentative and incomplete form. Someone was needed to clarify and edit them. His widow, Mary Fenollosa, had seen Pound's 'Contemporania' in *Poetry* and – through some instinctive, divining process – realized that Pound was the writer best equipped to deal with the spirit and breadth of her husband's work. She approached Pound; Pound agreed.

The Chinese Written Character
as a Medium for Poetry
BY
ERNEST FENOLLOSA

AN ARS POETICA

With a Foreword and Notes
BY
EZRA POUND

LONDON
STANLEY NOTT
FITZROY SQUARE

Title page to Pound's edition of Fenollosa's work, published in 1936. 'I should like', he wrote later, 'to protect Fenollosa from . . . the philologs who were impotent till Fen. showed the way (via y.v.t.) and who then swarmed in with inferior understandings.'

He started with Fenollosa's notes on Noh drama at the end of 1913 and did so, coincidentally, while in the company of Yeats. Yeats had asked Pound to be his secretary for three months, at a rural retreat suitable for prolonged composition, and Pound had written to his mother, 'My stay in Stone Cottage will not be in the least profitable . . . Yeats will amuse me part of the time and bore me to death with psychical research the rest. I regard the visit as a duty to posterity . . .' Despite his misgivings, however, he went. There is no doubt that Yeats valued his advice and companionship, especially during this vital period when Pound was discovering his own powers; Yeats might have thought that some of Pound's creative energy would be transferred to his own writings. He even put Pound, with Nietzsche, in early versions of *A Vision*, in the twelfth 'lunar phase' – both of them representing 'the Forerunner'. The older poet had written to Lady Gregory, '[Pound] helps me to get back to the definite and concrete away from modern abstractions. To talk over a poem with him is like getting you to put a sentence into dialect. All becomes clear and natural.'

Pound was later modestly to claim that he was merely passing on Ford Madox Ford's advice on such occasions, but whatever its

origins, Pound's role as a conveyor of ideas and information was an important one. Even his work on Fenollosa's manuscripts yielded surprising results; Yeats seized upon the tone and form of Noh drama, and revitalized them in the context of his own successful poetic dramas. Pound was rapidly becoming a vehicle for the age's most significant concerns. And he was only just beginning; while at Stone Cottage, Yeats suggested to Pound that he contact a promising young Irish writer whose work was as yet unpublished. His name was James Joyce.

Joyce was to exert a formative influence upon Pound, but it is a measure of Pound's critical perceptiveness – a perceptiveness in some ways close to clairvoyance – that he should immediately seize upon the significance of Joyce's work, and that he should act as his mentor and publicist for the next ten years. After Pound had written to him at Yeats's instigation, Joyce sent back a copy of *A Portrait of the Artist as a Young Man*. Pound had expected a few Imagist poems, and received something quite extraordinary instead. He wrote to Joyce, 'I'm not supposed to know much about prose but I think your novel is damn fine stuff – I dare say you know it quite as well as I do – clear and direct like Merimée . . . Confound it, I can't usually read prose at all,

A nest of poets at Newbuildings, January 1914, come to pay homage to Wilfrid Scawen Blunt. From left to right: Victor Plarr, T. Sturge Moore, W. B. Yeats, Wilfrid Blunt, Pound, Richard Aldington and F. S. Flint. A work by Gaudier-Brzeska was presented to Blunt.

Poet Who Will Wed

POET IN LOVE SONG EXTOLS HIS BRIDE

Ezra Pound, Wyncote Boy, Who Achieved Fame Abroad, Soon to Wed.

(Photo by Haeseler.)

Ezra Pound is a young man who went from Wyncote to England and there wrote poems of so much merit that he gained a special place in the highest literary circles. One of his writings led to a romance, a result of which is the announcement of his engagement to Miss Dorothy Shakespear, of London.

Phila. Poet in Stanza Tells of His Romance

Man's love follows many faces,
My love only one face knoweth;
Towards thee only my love floweth,
And outstrips the swift stream's paces.
Were this love well here displayed,
As flame flameth 'neath thin jade,
Love should glow through these, phrases.

Cable announcement of the coming marriage of Ezra Pound, the brilliant young Philadelphia poet, and Miss Dorothy Shakespear, daughter of Mr. and Mrs. Hope Shakespear, of London, the event to take place on Saturday April 18, and not on April 14, as first published, has attracted attention to the brilliant career of this youth, whose early days were spent at Wyncote, in the Old York Road section.

Pound has been haled in England as one of the world's great poets. Kipling has placed such an estimate on him, saying also that the young man's lyrical gifts are of the highest.

His romance has spurred the young author's Pegasus. It is sung in a canson, of which the stanza leading this article is a part. The poem is dedicated to Miss Shakespear and to her mother, Olivia Shakespear. Miss Shakespear's parents live in Brunswick Gardens, London, where the marriage will be solemnized. She is just past twenty. The romance spans several years.

Mother Proud of Poet.

Pound's parents are Mr. and Mrs. Homer L. Pound, whose home is at 166 Fernbrook Avenue, Wyncote. The young man's mother is naturally very proud of her son's career, and yesterday talked entertainingly of his life abroad.

not anybody's in English except James and Hudson and a little Conrad.' Pound began to publish *A Portrait*, in serial form, in *The Egoist* of February 1914; his struggle on Joyce's behalf had begun.

Now, just at the moment when his public role was about to assume another aspect, his private life took a new direction. He married Dorothy Shakespear, and they moved into a queer, triangular flat in Holland Park Chambers, Kensington. There is no doubt that, both before and after his marriage, Pound at least aspired towards promiscuity. Phyllis Bottome wrote in her autobiography, *From the Life*, 'The biology of sex was to the young Ezra a joyous discovery.' There was even a short verse, 'The Virgin's Prayer', going around London which Pound used to quote delightedly:

> Ezra Pound
> And Augustus John
> Bless the bed
> That I lie on.

But his marriage to Dorothy was the first permanent relationship of his life, and it was to endure – albeit in a tenuous and in the end melancholy form – until his death. Dorothy herself has been variously depicted, although Pound rarely mentions her in his work or in his published correspondence. She was called both saintly and naive; Wyndham Lewis described her as 'a good turncoat bourgeoisie [*sic*]'; to another friend of Pound's, Iris Barry, she resembled a 'young Victorian lady out skating'. She was quiet, she was devoted to Pound and seemed to appreciate his assorted company of writers and eccentrics. Indeed, she had artistic skills of her own, and was an accomplished painter. But her personality was always reserved and,

Opposite: An article from the *Philadelphia Press*, 26 March 1914, announcing Pound's engagement. The phrase, 'one of the world's great poets', may possibly have been suggested by the great poet himself.

The marriage certificate of Ezra and Dorothy Pound; they spent their honeymoon at Stone Cottage, where Pound continued with his work on Noh drama. His work, as always, came first.

PAGE 97

1914   **Marriage Solemnized at the Parish Church, in the Parish of Kensington, in the County of London.**

No.	When Married	Name and Surname	Age	Condition	Rank or Profession	Residence at the time of Marriage	Father's Name and Surname	Rank or Profession of Father
93	20th April 1914	Ezra Pound	28	Bachelor	M.A. Poet	5 Holland Place Chambers W.	Homer Loomis Pound	Assayer
		Dorothy Shakespear	27	Spinster	-	12 Brunswick Gardens W.	Henry Hope Shakespear	Solicitor

Married in the Parish Church, according to the Rites and Ceremonies of the Established Church, by or after *Banns*

By me *S. Groves*

This Marriage was Solemnized between us { Ezra Pound / Dorothy Shakespear } In the Presence of us { Hy Hope Shakespear / H. T. Tucker }

The above is a true Copy from the Registrar Book of Marriages in the Parish of KENSINGTON, in the County of LONDON.

as Witness my hand, this *Twentieth* day of *April* 1914

S.G.
CURATE AND REGISTRAR.

Right: Aldeburgh Boats, 1914, by Dorothy Shakespear. Her work has remained unjustifiably neglected. Her interest in small intensely perceived forms was at odds with his more grandiose concerns.

Below: A caricature of the Vorticists, Lewis, Gaudier-Brzeska and Pound. Lewis wrote: 'To the English eye, the period of *Blast* . . . will appear an island of incomprehensible bliss, dwelt in by strange shapes.'

THE LEWIS-BRZESKA-POUND TROUPE.
Blasting their own trumpets before the walls of Jericho.

in the language of contemporary cliché, 'buttoned-up'. It could not have been, for long, a satisfying marriage for either party. In the Thirties Pound was to say to Daniel Cory, George Santayana's secretary, 'I fell in love with a beautiful picture that never came alive.'

But he was never a man to be bothered excessively by such personal matters; he was quite incapable of introspection, and he had a large talent for forgetting or ignoring those private doubts and sentiments which so deeply affect other people. And anyway in 1914, the year of his marriage, he was far more preoccupied with public and artistic matters. He took a growing interest in politics, an ominous symptom of what was to come; under the influence of Gaudier-Brzeska, he wrote about the 'new sculpture'; he even challenged Lascelles Abercrombie, a reputable critic of the time, to a duel for writing in praise of Wordsworth; but, most important of all, he became involved with Vorticism and with its journal, *Blast*.

Vorticism was, according to Wyndham Lewis in *Blasting and Bombardiering*, 'a youth racket. It was Ezra who in the first place organised us willy-nilly into that. For he was never satisfied until everything was *organised*.' What Vorticism represented was, in fact, an umbrella large enough and strong enough to cover the work, theories and controversies of a small group of artists living together in London at the same time. The idea of a 'group' naturally appealed to Pound's conspiratorial instincts: '*Blast*,' he wrote, 'has behind it some of the best brains in England, a set of artists who know quite well what they want.' And so Pound became the movement's theorist, arranging elaborate aesthetic excuses for the work of Gaudier-Brzeska, Lewis, Edward Wadsworth, and for their presence together within the pages of one magazine.

Lewis, in *Time and Western Man*, has described Pound's role in less than revolutionary terms: 'What struck them [the *Blast* group] principally about Pound was that his fire-eating propagandist utterances were not accompanied by any very experimental efforts in his particular medium . . . Pound supplied the Chinese crackers, and a trayful of mild jokes for our paper; also much ingenious support in the

William Roberts's portrait of the Vorticists, at the Restaurant de la Tour Eiffel, London, spring 1915. Pound wrote of the Blast group: 'We worked separately, we found an underlying agreement, we decided to stand together.'

1

BLAST First (from politeness) **ENGLAND**

CURSE ITS CLIMATE FOR ITS SINS AND INFECTIONS

DISMAL SYMBOL, SET round our bodies,
of effeminate lout within.

VICTORIAN VAMPIRE, the **LONDON** cloud sucks
the **TOWN'S** heart.

A 1000 MILE LONG, 2 KILOMETER Deep

BODY OF WATER even, is pushed against us

from the Floridas, **TO MAKE US MILD.**

OFFICIOUS MOUNTAINS keep back **DRASTIC WINDS**

SO MUCH VAST MACHINERY TO PRODUCE

THE CURATE of "Eltham"
BRITANNIC ÆSTHETE
WILD NATURE CRANK
DOMESTICATED
POLICEMAN
LONDON COLISEUM
SOCIALIST-PLAYWRIGHT
DALY'S MUSICAL COMEDY
GAIETY CHORUS GIRL
TONKS

2

OH BLAST FRANCE

pig plagiarism
BELLY
SLIPPERS
POODLE TEMPER
BAD MUSIC

SENTIMENTAL GALLIC GUSH
SENSATIONALISM
FUSSINESS.

PARISIAN PAROCHIALISM. Complacent young man,
so much respect for Papa
and his son !—Oh !—Papa
is wonderful: but all papas
are !

BLAST

APERITIFS (Pernots, Amers picon)
Bad change
Naively seductive Houri salon-
picture Cocottes
Slouching blue porters (can
carry a pantechnicon)
Stupidly rapacious people at
every step
Economy maniacs
Bouillon Kub (for being a bad
pun)

---

english and american press.' Pound, in an essay on Vorticism, saw his 'Chinese' posture in rather different terms: 'As an active and informal association it might be said that Lewis supplied the volcanic force, Brzeska the animal energy, and perhaps that I contributed a certain Confucian calm and reserve.' Pound's capacity for self-deception here ('calm and reserved' he never was, and never could be) is symptomatic; it is not a hypocritical or selfish gesture – it is simply that he genuinely believed only what he wanted to believe, whatever the facts of the matter might be. It is not surprising, therefore, that Pound spoke very differently of Lewis and of *Blast* some thirty years later in a broadcast from Rome: '*Blast*, the word commonly meaning explosion of dynamite, etc., but connected in the arcane recesses of Mr Lewis's mind with blastoderms and sources of life . . . that manifesto marks the end of the Marxist era (if there was a Marxist era), marks the end of nineteenth century usurocracy and mercantilism.' For Pound, the important descriptions were those after the event; he lived in a perpetual present, in which all his earlier activities and theories were given a fresh and often novel significance in the light of whatever concerned him at the time.

But, despite this latter-day evangelism, Vorticism did have a real significance in Pound's England. Although it had been inspired by the spirit of Futurism and Cubism, its debt to these foreign sources was

Extracts from the manifestos in the first issue of *Blast*, 20 June 1914. It was printed on yellow pages and had shocking pink covers. The aim of *Blast*, Harriet Monroe commented in an editorial in *Poetry*, was 'to blow away, in thick black capitals half an inch high, the Victorian Vampire.'

Opposite: The cover of the second issue of *Blast* – and the last.

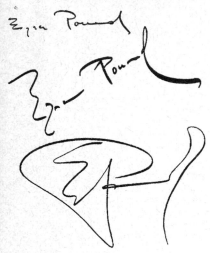

Pound's signatures – the first two written in 1909, and the third in 1933, which is looser, more like an ideogram. Note the connection between the final signature and Gaudier-Brzeska's designs of Pound's head, above.

largely unacknowledged; it was a specifically nationalist force. It marked the attempt to bring together modernist or revolutionary art within an English context, to harness the energies of the most interesting pre-War artists in an enterprising and serious way. For Pound, Vorticism also became the focal point for his increasingly complex perceptions about the nature of poetry. It represented, for him, an attempt to breathe a kind of heroic life into Imagism – to give the sharp but essentially static perceptions of the Imagists pace and epic breadth. Most importantly, Vorticism embodied the last attempt to comprehend, as a living unity, the forms of sculpture, poetry and painting. But the enterprise failed: the War intervened, and the vortex disappeared. Gaudier-Brzeska was killed; Pound and Lewis went separate ways, increasingly preoccupied with their own affairs. But their movement still haunts our own era; it represented at least the possibility of radical cultural change in England – although that promise was never in fact fulfilled.

Its effects at the time, however, made up in scandal for what they lacked in substance. The literary establishment was horrified by the tone and manner of *Blast*, and Ford Madox Ford described the ensuing fuss in *Thus to Revisit*:

For the London season of 1914 these young fellows not only drove the old – oh, the horribly wearisome! – Academics out of the field, the market and the forum; they created for themselves also a 'public' that had never looked at a book otherwise than to be bored with it; or considered that an Art was an interesting, inspiring or amusing appearance. That was extraordinarily valuable. And I believe that their influence at that date extended across the Atlantic itself and that there it still obtains.

Pound himself recounted, in one of his wartime broadcasts, how a copy of the Vorticist magazine had been left on the lawn of Sir Herbert Beerbohm-Tree's residence during a storm: 'Sir Herbert gazed elegiacally from the drawing room window on the scene of grass and wet dampness. A flash of lightning lit up the lawn; there in its solitude, huge on the flaring magenta cover, the word BLAST was written, in block letters, vividly effulgent.'

Certainly Vorticism hastened the process of Pound's social and cultural estrangement from the metropolitan establishment; his manner and his temperament had not endeared him to the literary world but, as long as he remained a tame lion of the salons and the writer of rather graceful contemporary verse, he was tolerated. But his association with Imagism and Vorticism, his increasingly direct poetry and his increasingly rebarbative criticism, had placed him right out of bounds. Aldington describes a dinner given by Harold Monro, an English poet and editor: '. . . Everyone was deploring Ezra and running him down. Finally I could stand it no longer. I stood up and said, "Ezra Pound has more vitality in his little finger than the lot of you put together."' This was in fact true, but Pound's energetic talents did not recommend themselves to his less able contemporaries. And Pound did not hesitate to strike back: the more fiercely he was

Portrait of Pound by Gaudier-Brzeska, 1913–14. Gaudier-Brzeska was, according to Pound, amused by 'my intellectual tiredness and exhaustion, my general scepticism and quietness'.

criticized, the more assiduously he seemed to provoke criticism. He became what he had always felt himself to be – an 'outsider'. But it was an honourable role, 'in a country in love with amateurs, in a country where the incompetent have such beautiful manners and personalities so fragile and charming, that one cannot bear to injure their feelings by the introduction of competent criticism' (*Poetry*, June 1914). But Pound was being too modest; he could bear to criticize. He had written for his recreations, in *Who's Who*, 'Searching *The Times* for evidences of almost incredible stupidity.' When something was false, or stupid, he tended to say so: 'I've got a right to be severe. For one man I strike there are ten to strike back at me. I stand exposed. It hits me in my dinner invitations, in my weekends, in reviews of my own work. Nevertheless it's a good fight.'

Overleaf
Gaudier-Brzeska's last testament, from the trenches. Pound wrote after his death: 'We have lost the best of the young sculptors and the most promising. The arts will incur no worse loss from the war than this.'

VORTEX GAUDIER-BRZESKA.

(Written from the Trenches).

NOTE.—The sculptor writes from the French trenches, having been in the firing line since early in the war.

In September he was one of a patrolling party of twelve, seven of his companions fell in the fight over a roadway.

In November he was nominated for sergeancy and has been since slightly wounded, but expects to return to the trenches.

He has been constantly employed in scouting and patrolling and in the construction of wire entanglements in close contact with the Boches.

I HAVE BEEN FIGHTING FOR TWO MONTHS and I can now gauge the intensity of Life.

HUMAN MASSES teem and move, are destroyed and crop up again.

HORSES are worn out in three weeks, die by the roadside.

DOGS wander, are destroyed, and others come along.

WITH ALL THE DESTRUCTION that works around us NOTHING IS CHANGED, EVEN SUPERFICIALLY. LIFE IS THE SAME STRENGTH, THE MOVING AGENT THAT PERMITS THE SMALL INDIVIDUAL TO ASSERT HIMSELF.

THE BURSTING SHELLS, the volleys, wire entanglements, projectors, motors, the chaos of battle DO NOT ALTER IN THE LEAST, the outlines of the hill we are besieging. A company of PARTRIDGES scuttle along before our very trench.

IT WOULD BE FOLLY TO SEEK ARTISTIC EMOTIONS AMID THESE LITTLE WORKS OF OURS.

THIS PALTRY MECHANISM, WHICH SERVES AS A PURGE TO OVER-NUMEROUS HUMANITY.

THIS WAR IS A GREAT REMEDY.

IN THE INDIVIDUAL IT KILLS ARROGANCE, SELF-ESTEEM, PRIDE.

IT TAKES AWAY FROM THE MASSES NUMBERS UPON NUMBERS OF UNIMPORTANT UNITS, WHOSE ECONOMIC ACTIVITIES BECOME NOXIOUS AS THE RECENT TRADE CRISES HAVE SHOWN US.

MY VIEWS ON SCULPTURE REMAIN ABSOLUTELY THE SAME,

IT IS THE VORTEX OF WILL, OF DECISION, THAT BEGINS.

I SHALL DERIVE MY EMOTIONS SOLELY FROM THE ARRANGE-MENT OF SURFACES, I shall present my emotions by the ARRANGEMENT OF MY SURFACES, THE PLANES AND LINES BY WHICH THEY ARE DEFINED.

Just as this hill where the Germans are solidly entrenched, gives me a nasty feeling, solely because its gentle slopes are broken up by earth-works, which throw long shadows at sunset. Just so shall I get feeling, of whatsoever definition, from a statue ACCORDING TO ITS SLOPES, varied to infinity.

I have made an experiment. Two days ago I pinched from an enemy a mauser rifle. Its heavy unwieldy shape swamped me with a powerful IMAGE of brutality.

I was in doubt for a long time whether it pleased or displeased me.

I found that I did not like it.

I broke the butt off and with my knife I carved in it a design, through which I tried to express a gentler order of feeling, which I preferred.

BUT I WILL EMPHASIZE that MY DESIGN got its effect (just as the gun had) FROM A VERY SIMPLE COMPOSITION OF LINES AND PLANES.

GAUDIER-BRZESKA.

MORT POUR LA PATRIE.

Henri Gaudier-Brzeska: after months of fighting and two promotions for gallantry Henri Gaudier-Brzeska was killed in a charge at Neuville St. Vaast, on June 5th, 1915.

Dorothy Shakespear's design for the cover of the *Catholic Anthology*, edited by Pound and published in 1915. The anthology is chiefly remarkable as the first appearance in a book of T. S. Eliot's poetry.

Opposite

Portraits by Wyndham Lewis. *Above left:* T. S. Eliot. Eliot said of Pound: 'He would cajole and almost coerce other men into writing well so that he often presented the appearance of a man trying to convey to a very deaf person the fact that the house is on fire.' *Above right:* James Joyce. Pound wrote of him, in this year, to William Carlos Williams, as 'the innocent Joyce (non-conformist parson from Aberdeen)'. *Below left:* Pound. '*Always*', Lewis wrote, 'in appearance the Westerner in excelsis.'

Below right: Wyndham Lewis. Pound wrote: 'The vitality, the fullness of the man! Nobody knows it.'

It was indeed a good fight, and increasingly the best were coming onto his side. In September 1914, for example, on the advice of a mutual friend, Conrad Aiken ('Pound seemed to me then the most exciting thing going,' he wrote later), Thomas Stearns Eliot, a young American recently arrived in London, went to visit his more illustrious contemporary. They chatted and found that, although Eliot thought very little of Pound's earlier work ('His verse is touchingly incompetent,' he wrote to Aiken), they had a great deal in common. Both of them were expatriates, and both of them were possessed by the idea of history and of the European tradition. Both of them were, in a sense, refugees.

A week after their first meeting, Eliot sent Pound a copy of 'The Love Song of J. Alfred Prufrock'; and Pound wrote at once to Harriet Monroe in Chicago: 'I was jolly well right about Eliot. He has sent in the best poem I have yet had or seen from an American. PRAY GOD IT BE NOT A SINGLE AND UNIQUE SUCCESS.' And so the strange friendship and collaboration began; Pound adopted Eliot in an almost paternal fashion. He published his work in *Blast*, *Poetry* and in the *Catholic Anthology*. Since Joyce was not in England to be exhibited, Eliot became Pound's prize possession. Wyndham Lewis, in *Blasting and Bombardiering*, has described the two of them together: 'Ezra now lay flung back in a typical posture of aggressive ease . . . However, he kept steadily beneath his quizzical but self-satisfied observation his latest prize, or discovery – the author of Prufrock.'

The taciturn author of 'Prufrock' was greatly revived as a result. Pound's enthusiasm for his work cleared his lethargic depression about the nature of his poetry, and Pound's steady prompting kept him writing. He insisted that Eliot become a serious and professional poet. And, as Wyndham Lewis put it, 'Mr Eliot was lifted out of his lunar alley-ways and fin-de-siècle nocturnes into a massive region of verbal creation in contact with that astonishing didactic intelligence, that is all.' No observer could have guessed that, in the end, it was Eliot who would become the apparent master of contemporary poetry – and that he would, indirectly, save Pound's reputation and perhaps even his life.

And so, by 1915, Pound had gathered around himself a number of poets and artists who were the proper objects of his missionary zeal and energy. Pound described England, during this period, as 'the center of Awakening', and he wrote to Harriet Monroe in January 1915, 'My problem is to keep alive a certain group of advancing poets, to set the arts in their rightful place as the acknowledged guide and lamp of civilization.' Eliot, therefore, was published and encouraged; and, at the same time, Pound was acting as an unpaid literary agent for James Joyce. He fought hard, but at first unsuccessfully, for the publication of *A Portrait of the Artist as a Young Man*; he engineered funds and grants in response to Joyce's occasionally petulant requests; and he enlisted the help of John Quinn in discovering money and publishers for Joyce in America. Pound was, in other words, busy – and he loved it. Herbert Read met him in this year: 'I took away the

portrait of
T. S. Eliot.
Wyndham Lewis.

WL.
1920.

Drawing of James Joyce. 1920.
by Wyndham Lewis.

Wyndham Lewis 1920.
portrait of Ezra Pound

impression of an agile lynx, beautiful in features, aggressively dressed, who sprang from conversational point to point.'

The 1914–1918 War hardly seemed to have touched Pound yet, but it emerges, indirectly, in a volume of his 'translations' which appeared in 1915. *Cathay* was adapted from Ernest Fenollosa's notes on Chinese poetry, and Pound completed the bulk of the work in the first weeks of the War. He had sent some of the poems to Gaudier-Brzeska, then fighting in the trenches in France, and the sculptor had written back that 'the poems depict our situation in a wonderful way':

> Here we are, picking the first fern-shoots
> And saying: When shall we get back to our country?

Eliot described Pound, as a result of this volume, as the 'inventor of Chinese poetry for our time'. But *Cathay* represents more than this since, in its firmness of image and hardness of outline, it achieves a quite new thing in English poetry. Its eloquence comes from the clarity of its statements rather than from sentiment or rhetorical glissades; it pins down precisely, with a kind of brutal lyricism, the nature of anxiety, loss and regret. But it does so by description rather than association, by direct images rather than analogies:

> What is the use of talking, and there is no end of
>   talking,
> There is no end of things in the heart.
> I call in the boy,
> Have him sit on his knees here
>   To seal this,
> And send it a thousand miles, thinking.

The straightforwardness of this language has its own peculiar resonance; there had been nothing quite like it before. In fact Pound's creative writing was now beginning to acquire its own inner momentum. By the middle of December 1915 he had completed *Three Cantos*, as yet a slightly ramshackle sequence and soon to be extensively revised. But the dream of the 'long poem', which had been with him since his adolescence in America, was now becoming actual. His immediate financial prospects, however, weren't quite so promising: his earnings in 1915 amounted to £42 10s. 0d.

By 1916 Pound was almost alone in London. Joyce was in Paris. Lewis had gone to the front, and the War itself had finally affected Pound personally with the death of Gaudier-Brzeska. Charles Olson wrote later, 'It was as though Pound had never got over it, that Gaudier's death is the source of his hate for contemporary England and America.' In his friends' absence, whether temporary or permanent, Pound busied himself about their critical reputations. He serialized Lewis's novel, *Tarr*, in *The Egoist*, and tried hard but unsuccessfully to have it published. He wrote extensively, and often, in praise of Joyce's work, and obtained for him a grant from the Civil List. He completed his study of Gaudier-Brzeska's sculpture. He was endlessly

GAUDIER-BRZESKA

A MEMOIR

BY

EZRA POUND

WITH 4 PORTRAITS & 34 ILLUSTRATIONS
REPRODUCTIONS OF SCULPTURE AND
DRAWINGS BY THE ARTIST

Crown 4to. 12s. 6d. net

LONDON : JOHN LANE, THE BODLEY HEAD, W.
NEW YORK : JOHN LANE COMPANY   MCMXVI

reviewing, 'puffing', quarrelling. Iris Barry wrote, 'No one was ever busier, gayer . . . seeing everything, meeting everybody, full of the latest gossip . . . making strange sounds and cries in his talking but otherwise quite formal and extremely polite.' She also noted that in 1916 'his name stood in England, along with that of the sculptor Epstein, for all that was dangerously different, horridly new'. And Carl Sandburg, the American poet, recorded, in this year, 'All talk of modern poetry, by people who know, ends with dragging in Ezra Pound somewhere.' Pound was becoming a 'personality', a presence which could not go unnoticed.

But it was also a frustrating time for him. He still could not get *Tarr* or Joyce's *A Portrait* published, and he was running into difficulties with his own new book of poetry, *Lustra*. This volume was considered by its publisher, Elkin Mathews, to be in parts too obscene. After a great deal of argument, Pound was compelled to delete certain poems from the standard edition: '. . . The dam'd bloody insidious way one is edged into these tacit hypocrisies *is* disgusting,' he wrote to Harriet Monroe. The book itself now seems disciplined and ironic, with the novel directness of *Cathay* matched by an astonishing formal clarity:

> Like a skein of loose silk blown against a wall
> She walks by the railing of a path in Kensington Gardens,
>
> And she is dying piece-meal
> of a sort of emotional anaemia.

This directness, bordering on assertiveness, derives from the fact that Pound had at last constructed a language in which he could write and think. The confidence of *Lustra* comes from Pound's sense of his own powers – a sense which had hitherto eluded him. In this volume he went beyond his influences for the first time, with a measured abruptness of diction that perfectly matched his own temperament and the quality of his perceptions:

> The apparition of these faces in the crowd;
> Petals on a wet, black bough.

But the struggles with Elkin Mathews over the book, and his growing isolation from the English 'world of letters', had begun to sour him. 'It is wonderful', J. B. Yeats (the poet's father) wrote to John Quinn in 1917, 'how people hate him. But hatred is the harvest he wants to gather.' A pattern was now in fact emerging in Pound's literary career; he needed conflict, and everything was being turned into a series of confrontations – with himself, with his contemporaries, and with 'the system'.

And so for the next two years, until the end of the War, he led the life of a belligerent critical propagandist. In March 1917 he became the London editor of *The Little Review*, an American journal run by Margaret Anderson and Jane Heap, two editors of uncompromising judgment who published Eliot, Williams, Yeats and Joyce. Pound had written to Margaret Anderson, 'I want an "official organ" (vile

L U S T R A
of Ezra Pound
with Earlier Poems

For Private Circulation
Sixty Copies Printed.   New York, October 1917.
This is Number___

Title page to *Lustra*, the unexpurgated edition which Elkin Mathews refused to print because it contained some 'very nasty' poems. This American edition was in fact subsidized by John Quinn.

Opposite: Pound's editorial in the May 1917 issue of *The Little Review*, a literary periodical edited by Margaret Anderson and Jane Heap. 'I must', he had written to Margaret Anderson, 'have a steady place for my best stuff.'

The Little Review

VOL. IV.   MAY 1917   NO. I

Editorial

Ezra Pound

I HAVE accepted the post of Foreign Editor of *The Little Review:* chiefly because:

I.

I wished a place where the current prose writings of James Joyce, Wyndham Lewis, T. S. Eliot, and myself might appear regularly, promptly, and together, rather than irregularly, sporadically, and after useless delays.

My connection with *The Little Review* does not imply a severance of my relations with *Poetry* for which I still remain Foreign Correspondent, and in which my poems will continue to appear until its guarantors revolt.

I would say, however, in justification both of *Poetry* and myself, that *Poetry* has never been "the instrument" of my "radicalism". I respect Miss Monroe for all that she has done for the support of American poetry, but in the conduct of her magazine my voice and vote have always been the vote and voice of a minority.

I recognize that she, being "on the ground", may be much better fitted to understand the exigencies of magazine publishing in America, but *Poetry* has done numerous things to which I could never have given my personal sanction, and which could not have occurred in any magazine which had constituted itself my "instrument". *Poetry* has shown an unflagging courtesy to a lot of old fools and fogies whom I should have told to go to hell *tout pleinement* and *bonnement*. It has refrained from attacking a number of public nuisances; from implying that the personal charm of the late Mr. Gilder need not have been,

phrase). I mean I want a place where I and T. S. Eliot can appear once a month (or once an "issue") and where Joyce can appear when he likes, and where Wyndham Lewis can appear if he comes back from the War.' His work on behalf of this triad was heroic; he was a kind of literary government in *their* exile. He reviewed Joyce's work on every occasion he could, finally pushed *A Portrait* into book form, and started to serialize *Ulysses* in *The Little Review* in 1918. He also worked closely with Eliot during these years, publishing his work in *Poetry* and *The Egoist*, and managed finally to bring out *Prufrock and Other Observations* through the agency of the Egoist Press: 'As a matter of fact,' he wrote to John Quinn in November 1917, 'I have borrowed the cost of the printing bill (very little) and am being The Egoist. But Eliot don't know it . . .'

Ford Madox Ford has described Pound's extraordinary energy and industry on behalf of others during these years: 'A great vitality: an immense heroism. And it is a beautiful heroism since it has been so persisted in and has remained so without reward or applause.' Although in later life Pound's enthusiasms were often to spring from personal contact rather than disinterested perception, during this period he seems to have divined the essential nature of modern literature and then acted upon his intuitions. He treated his protégés, according to Eliot, 'almost impersonally, as art or literature machines to be carefully tended and oiled for the sake of their potential output.' The impersonal sense of urgency, however uncomfortable it might have been for others, derived from this instinctive belief in his own critical judgment. And his judgment was not misplaced.

It could be said, in fact, that Pound created the taste of an entire literary generation; if it had not been for his efforts, the work of Eliot and Joyce might well have remained obscure or little known. Pound put the essential point himself, in an essay in *The Egoist* in 1917: 'The last few years have seen the gradual shaping of a party of intelligence, a party not bound by any central doctrine or theory . . . I would say that James Joyce produces the nearest thing to Flaubertian prose that we now have in English, just as Wyndham Lewis has written a novel which is more like, and more fitly compared with, Dostoievski than is the work of any of his contemporaries. In like manner, Mr T. S. Eliot comes nearer to filling the place of Jules Laforgue in our generation.'

This, although by no means Pound's last word on the three men, marks the crowning point of his entrepreneurial career. His judgment was not to be so sharp or so intense in later years, and in any event he was soon to turn his missionary zeal to matters other than literary. There were more immediate problems which began to affect him: having tended to the work of others, he now found the time to worry about his own poetry – which seemed to lack impetus and direction. By 1918, also, he had become almost entirely disenchanted with the commercial publishing system in England and with the whole 'tone' of London culture. But, as always, he found a way of externalizing – and objectifying – his private unease; just at this moment, he met the economic theorist, Major C. H. Douglas, whose doctrine of Social

Opposite: James Joyce, *c.* 1934. Pound wrote of Joyce some years later: '. . . to best of my recollection he never alluded to any of his eng/ & am/ contemporaries as writers'.

Credit confirmed and explained Pound's rising disgust at the commercial systems of 'art' in England. In fact, Social Credit was unfortunately to become Pound's next great cause.

Its doctrine states, quite simply, that once money has lost its natural basis in people's needs and aspirations – when, in other words, it has been turned into a commodity merely to be bought and sold – then the nation and its culture sour. Money is a complex measure of man's time and the worth of his labour; when it becomes an anonymous entity to be hoarded and manipulated, all other human and social values shift downward. But there was also a blindingly simple economic point to be made in this connection: the bankers control money at the expense of everyone else in the community. By withholding money, they can ensure that there is not enough credit to buy goods; an absurd lacuna develops between national production and national wealth: 'The purchasing power of the whole people can never catch up with the price of the goods that they bring into being,' he wrote in *Social Credit: an Impact*. Human want is thus artificially created, because money is no longer able to fulfil its original purpose as a measure of what has been laboured and achieved.

This is, of course, somewhat to simplify the major doctrines of Social Credit – although Pound himself simplified them from the beginning. There are many reasons why this particular set of ideas appealed so strongly to him. It offered a readily comprehensible solution to a complex problem; it confirmed Pound's obsession with 'origins', with the need for true, basic values: '. . . A national currency can be a true register of wealth only when the amount of money in circulation corresponds to the wealth of the natural resources known to exist in that nation's land and in the known appetites of its citizens,' he was to write later. But, more importantly, Social Credit exactly complemented Pound's own aesthetic theories. Just as he had defined Imagism as a return to the direct and simple treatment of the word, without artificial supports or rhetorical manipulation, so C. H. Douglas suggested that the same systematic constraints be removed from a nation's money and its goods.

But Social Credit may also have appealed to Pound's naive and dogmatic populism, which considered the woes of mankind to be the product of some shadowy system conspiring against the individual – a system likely to be manipulated by financiers and Jews. Douglas's attacks against these faceless men, the boards of bankers and usurers who acquire and use money for their own ends, exactly corresponded to Pound's growing sense of displacement and paranoia in England. The 'system' there was certainly against him.

Indeed by the end of the War he had become uncharacteristically withdrawn and dismissive. New faces and new movements were emerging; he was understood and appreciated by a steadily diminishing band of writers, despite all his journalistic efforts. It was during this period that he wrote the *Hell Cantos*, a sustained and vicious attack upon English culture:

The saccharescent, lying in glucose,
the pompous in cotton wool
with a stench like the fats at Grasse . . .

When Richard Aldington, now returned from the War, went to see
Pound, most of the energy and exuberance had gone: 'I found him
still in the same small apartment in Kensington . . . he kept tapping
his Adam's apple and assuring me that the English stopped short
there.' He meant, of course, that the English no longer had any brains
– a sense of grievance connected, Aldington assumed, with the fact
that 'at this time appreciation of Ezra's work had diminished to a pin-
prick'.

The diagnosis is true, although the situation itself was unjustified.
In fact one of Pound's great poems of the period, *Homage to Sextus
Propertius*, published in *Poetry*, elicited nothing more substantial than
casual brickbats from classical scholars who made fun of Pound's
rather loose translation of Propertius. Pound himself had conceived of
the poem in less narrow terms, as the record 'of certain emotions as
vital to me in 1917, faced with the infinite and ineffable imbecility of
the British Empire as they were to Propertius some centuries earlier,
when faced with the infinite and ineffable imbecility of the Roman
Empire.' But this was simply its context; the work itself is
elegant, lucid, with the tough certainty of a language that hits its
mark.

Pound's translations have often been considered to be his major
achievement. This is an overstatement, but it does contain an element
of critical justice. He often elicits great poetry from the manipulation
of another's voice, an external set of tones and circumstances which
are close enough to his own to be applied without syntactical discom-
fort. His restless and shifting identity found refuge only in a poetry of
polished surfaces; he could supply those surfaces, with his technical
and rhythmic expertise, and, when the interior could be passed off as
someone else's (as that of Propertius, for example), he was safe.

Homage to Sextus Propertius was condemned out of hand. In fact,
nothing Pound did now was praised. A collection of his most recent
work, *Quia Pauper Amavi* (1919), was unfavourably reviewed – except
for a piece by Eliot in *The Athenaeum* which Pound likened to 'granite
wreaths, leaden laurels'. His own work on the *Cantos*, which had been
continuing fitfully since 1915, seemed to be getting nowhere; his
enthusiasm and inspiration were waning. Even his prose works,
published in books of essays in both England and the United States,
found only a tiny audience. 'And now there is no longer any
intellectual *life* in England save what centres in this eight by ten
pentagonal room,' he wrote to William Carlos Williams in September
1920.

Pound's insecurity and restlessness fed off each other; he travelled
to Paris, Provence, Sirmione (where he met Joyce for the first time:
'Joyce pleasing, after the first shell of cantankerous Irishman', he
wrote to Quinn), and then back to Paris. By 1920, also, he had written
Hugh Selwyn Mauberley which was, according to Pound, 'the definite

attempt to get the novel cut down to the size of verse'. But the poem, because of its ambiguity and deliberate thinness of texture, does not seem to me quite the major achievement it is often claimed as being. It was written as a farewell to London culture, but it is marked at the same time by uncertainty and by Pound's distrust of his own powers during this period. What survives within it, and what makes it readable still, is Pound's sense of harmony. He had an astonishing ear for rhythmic movement, and it was one which never deserted him:

> Tell her that goes
> With song upon her lips
> But sings not out the song, nor knows
> The maker of it, some other mouth,
> May be as fair as hers,
> Might, in new ages, gain her worshippers,
> When our two dusts with Waller's shall be laid,
> Siftings on siftings in oblivion,
> Till change hath broken down
> All things save Beauty alone.

In this same period Pound also wrote *Indiscretions*, a quasi-mythical account of his family and his childhood, as though at this point, more than any other previously, he needed to return to his 'roots' – even if that meant inventing them. Then, in December 1920, Ezra and Dorothy Pound left for France; Pound himself had left England for ever. Nothing remained for him to do there and, after twelve years of activity and controversy, there was very little left to say. He had already met Cocteau, in 1919, and they had both been much impressed by each other. Perhaps, Pound thought, Paris could become a centre for his endeavours; perhaps that city, rather than London, could sustain a new cultural vortex.

Pound moved on with a sense of euphoria; he had already described Paris as 'a paradise for artists', and he sought there 'the triple extract of literature for export purposes . . . a poetic serum to save English letters from post-mature and American letters from premature suicide and decomposition' (*The Dial*, October 1920). Some months after he first arrived, he wrote that the poets and artists of Paris 'are without humbug, without jealousy and without an eye on any market whatsoever'. Even in later life, when Pound was apt to reverse his assessments of people and places, Paris still held a small place in his affections: 'Paris was tired, very tired, but they wanted *table rase*, they wanted the dead things cleared out even if there was nothing to replace them' (*Jefferson and/or Mussolini*). The implicit comparison here is with a deliquescent London. Pound had in fact told Sylvia Beach, the American bookseller living in Paris, that he and Dorothy had been obliged to flee London 'because the water was creeping up, and they might wake up some morning to find they had web feet'.

Now, however, they were waking up to an apparently new world. Joyce had moved to Paris in 1920, and here also were the artists

Opposite: A watercolour of Sirmione by Dorothy Shakespear.

Left: Jean Cocteau, 1926. Pound wrote to a literary disciple: 'Read Cocteau (I spose you do anyhow); read more if you haven't read all of him.' He was, indeed, one of the reasons why Pound left London and travelled to Paris.

Right: Francis Picabia, the French writer and painter. Pound had once described him as 'froth' but, having taken up residence in Paris, quickly changed his mind. 'Picabia', he said later, 'is the man who ties the knots in Picasso's tail.'

whom Pound saw as constituting a new 'awakening'. He wrote on his first arrival, 'Find Cocteau and Picabia intelligent. Fools abound but are less in one's way here.' Pound had indeed warmed to Picabia's work, having taken the precaution of meeting him first. But he seems to have lost his habit of total absorption in another's cause, and his own poetry was never again to be postponed or forgotten for the sake of someone else's art. The French writers, in any case, were not as interesting as the American or the English. Pound's review of Cocteau's *Poésies*, for example, is significant principally for the light which it throws on the development of Pound's own poetry: 'In a city the visual impressions succeed each other, overlap, overcross, they are "cinematographic" but they are not a simple, linear sequence. They are often a flood of nouns without verbal relations' (*The Dial*, January 1921). The escape from London released a fresh sense of life in him, and his creative energies revived under the bombardment of new people and new impressions.

Paris in the early Twenties was also full of music: Ravel, Stravinsky and Virgil Thomson were there; Copland was soon to arrive. Pound was himself something of an expert on music – he had written music criticism for *The New Age* under the pen-name of 'William Atheling' – and could settle down comfortably amongst them, at least for a while.

Detail of a painting of Tristan Tzara, the Dadaist poet, by Robert Delaunay. Pound became attached to Dadaism on his arrival in Paris, but he was more intrigued by its atmosphere of literary gossip than its actual achievements.

He moved with Dorothy into 70 *bis* rue Notre Dame des Champs, a flat filled with furniture which he had made himself, true to his belief in the virtues of practicality. Pound's interest in music was particularly directed toward the interrelation of words and music; he was at work on *Le Testament*, an opera based upon Villon's poem, which he had begun desultorily in London. But in Paris, also, there were literary cliques vying for attention, and Pound caught the old scent of intrigue and gossip which he had missed in his last years in London; he met Tristan Tzara and Louis Aragon, and for a time he became attached to the Dadaist movement. Vorticism, after all, was now dead and, anyway, that had been in another country. Dadaism (although it represented the destruction of the literary and cultural traditions which Pound had tried painstakingly to build) was the coming thing. He wrote in the Dadaist journal, *391*, 'Why Paris? Paris is the center of the world – why?' The question was meant to be rhetorical.

Indeed, everyone seemed to be coming to this new 'center'. Quinn, now playing a less prominent role in Pound's life, arrived; e. e. cummings was there; even Wyndham Lewis came, and thought Pound much improved: 'He was much more in his element in Paris. I actually believe he cooked better in Paris than he did in London.' Other expatriates, however, had different impressions of the man. A young American editor, Alfred Kreymborg, wrote in his autobiography, *Troubadour*, that although Pound still looked and sounded the quintessential American, 'There was never any doubt as to his contempt for the land of his birth . . . but he seemed ill at ease, even in Paris, although he had been accepted by many of the younger Parisians.'

Despite his new location, light years away from Kensington, Pound had not forgotten his old obligations. And it says much for his critical stamina and acumen that, although he was immersed in new movements and new people, he was still able to work productively on what, paradoxically, may be considered one of his major achievements: T. S. Eliot's *The Waste Land*. In November 1921 Eliot passed through Paris; he was on his way back to London from Lausanne, where he had been convalescing after a nervous collapse. He showed the typescript of the as yet incomplete poem to Pound who, immediately and characteristically, began work on editing it. The two men corresponded. Pound's editorial notes were always to the point: 'Phlebas is an integral part of the poem; the card pack introduces him, the drowned phoen. sailor. And he is needed ABSolootly where he is. Must stay in.' Eliot, on this and other points, accepted his advice.

The transformation of *The Waste Land* effected by Pound is, although not total, nevertheless remarkable. What had been a longer, more sustained and more elaborately lyrical work was changed into something less personal, tighter and more abrupt. It was precisely these qualities which were to lend the poem its air of modernity – since, in large part, our notion of what is 'modern' is derived from Pound's work and criticism. But these were not qualities which, in the end, suited Eliot, and he returned to his more personal and elegiac mode. Pound was to say later of his work: 'We mowed the grass for him, so that he could set up his doll house.' At any rate, Pound now thought the poem a success. In December 1921 he wrote to Eliot, 'Complimenti, you bitch. I am wracked by the seven jealousies.' Eliot was, and remained, deeply grateful for his textual emendations: he dedicated *The Waste Land* to 'Ezra Pound, il miglior fabbro.'

During this period, Pound continued with his interrupted work on the *Cantos*; by May 1922 he had completed the eighth canto, largely concerned with the presentation of mythical metamorphosis, which was to become the second canto. In fact, Pound was engaged in a complete revision of the cantos he had already written. In London his work on them had been desultory and uncertain, but this new enthusiasm is not difficult to explain. Paris was not as debilitating as London, in the end, had been – there were fewer distractions, so he could concentrate on the work in hand. But, more importantly, his ideas about the nature of the long poem were now coming into sharper focus.

It is significant in this connection that, by 1922, his two most important contemporaries had completed long and major works. Joyce had already published *Ulysses*, and *The Waste Land* was to come out at the end of the year. Pound's close reading of both works

e. e. cummings, the American poet whom Pound befriended in Paris. They remained close; when Pound was incarcerated in St Elizabeth's, cummings wrote in his defence: 'Every artist's strictly illimitable country is himself.'

Above: Ford Madox Ford, James Joyce, Pound and John Quinn in Pound's Paris studio in 1923. Pound, however, was soon to leave the old gang behind.

Left: Pound in his Paris studio, 1923, sitting on a chair he had made. George Antheil, who met Pound in this year, described him as 'a ridiculous Don Quixote'.

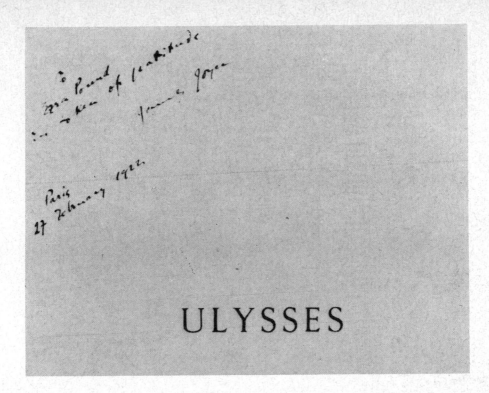

ULYSSES

undoubtedly affected his own continuing struggle with the *Cantos*. And although it would be unwise to claim that either work had any major impact on the final shape of Pound's poem, it is clear, for example, that Joyce's own assiduity in the service of his art, and the epic scope which *Ulysses* encompassed, made a profound impression upon him. In fact it was shortly after Sylvia Beach, under the imprint of Shakespeare & Company, had published Joyce's novel, that Pound sat down to his most serious meditation on the shape and content of the *Cantos*. By the summer of 1922 he had roughed out a draft of the material which was to appear in the first volume, and he wrote to his old teacher, Felix Schelling, in July, 'The first 11 cantos are preparation of the palette. I *have to* get down all the colours or elements I want for the poem. Some perhaps too enigmatically and abbreviatedly. I hope, heaven help me, to bring them into some sort of design and architecture later . . .'

A new self-confidence now set in. He announced, during one of his restless wanderings, to Italy in 1922, that the Christian Era was over and that the 'Pound Era' had begun. He was even able successfully to adopt the pose of the middle-aged man above the cultural battles which swirled around him. He stayed on amiable enough terms with other American expatriates, but he was not a serious drinker or smoker, and 'the lost generation' did not appeal to him. Only with Ernest Hemingway did he strike up a firm friendship; Hemingway taught him how to box, and he tried to teach Hemingway how to write. They

James Joyce's inscription to Pound in the first edition of *Ulysses*. Pound had already published sections of the novel in *The Little Review*, and remained its most effective propagandist.

Opposite: Sylvia Beach, the American who ran Shakespeare & Company, the bookshop in Paris. 'In the course of his conversations', she wrote, 'he [Pound] did boast, but of carpentry. He asked me if there was anything around the shop that needed mending.'

Opposite: Ernest Hemingway in Paris, 1924. He was Pound's closest friend there – more than anyone Pound taught him 'how to write and how not to write'.

Left: Notice of a concert on 11 December 1923 given by Olga Rudge and George Antheil at which works by Antheil and Pound were performed. Pound, in his critical writings, described harmony as 'lifeless' and concentrated instead upon the energetic properties of rhythm and time – as in his poetry.

Right: Olga Rudge, a violinist who was never willing to play second fiddle.

even toured Italian battlefields together in 1923 – a triumph of the *machismo* which Hemingway possessed and which Pound aspired to. Hemingway described him in a characteristically abbreviated fashion: 'Ezra Pound devotes one fifth of his working time to writing poetry . . . With the rest of the time he tries to advance the future, both material and artistic, of his friends . . . Personally he is tall, has a patchy red beard, fine eyes, strange haircuts and is very shy. Many people hate him, and he plays a fine game of tennis. He would live much longer if he did not eat so fast.'

There was another American in Paris, with whom Pound was soon on much more intimate terms. He met a young violinist, Olga Rudge, at a Paris recital in 1922. She was a fine musician and, according to one observer, 'a dark, pretty, Irish-looking girl about 25 years old'. The attraction was mutual and immediate – they became lovers. It is unlikely that Pound consulted his wife's feelings in the matter, but she seems to have endured her husband's infidelity with great restraint throughout her life. Indeed this early incident set a pattern in Pound's emotional career. Dorothy, after all, would always be there; he felt free to find more inspiring and less 'bourgeois' company elsewhere.

There were other reasons why Pound was busy in Paris; his old missionary enthusiasms had not entirely vanished, and in June 1923 he managed to discover someone new and potentially interesting. George Antheil was a young American composer whose abrupt and discontinuous work seemed to Pound to be an attempt to do in music what the Vorticists had done in art: 'In the series of six piano pieces called "Sonate sauvage",' he wrote, 'Antheil gives us the first music really suggesting Lewis's "Timon" designs.' Antheil was at first flattered, and his ambitions were aroused: 'Ezra had previously bludgeoned his way into a number of musical salons,' he confessed later in his autobiography, *Bad Boy of Music*, 'moreover he was a very good friend of Jean Cocteau, who was then the high priest of all modern French artistic endeavour.' But there was a slight ambiguity in this potentially fruitful friendship: 'From the first day I met him Ezra was never to have the slightest idea of what I was really after in music. I honestly don't think he wanted to have. I think he merely wanted to use me as a whip with which to lash out at all those who disagreed with him, particularly Anglo-Saxons.'

When Sylvia Beach told Antheil that Pound was about to write a book about his music and its theoretical context, the prospect 'scared' him. But in fact, although *Antheil and the Treatise on Harmony* may be impetuous or naive in parts, the text itself is a serious and comprehensible examination of what Pound considered to be the 'new music'. It is not, in any case, every young composer whose work is celebrated in book form, and Antheil admitted that 'after Ezra Pound wrote his book about me, the entire Anglo-American literary set became interested'.

And Pound was in turn still interested in what he called 'the really important Paris that matters'; he was seen everywhere and with everyone, and was as a consequence someone to be feared, respected or consciously snubbed. Gertrude Stein, whom Pound met in 1923, did a little of all three. Pound visited her, lectured her on her own collection of paintings and, in his eagerness to explain, toppled out of her favourite armchair. Miss Stein has left a description of the occasion in *The Autobiography of Alice B. Toklas*: 'He came home to dinner with us and he stayed and he talked about Japanese prints among other things. Gertrude Stein liked him but did not find him amusing. She said he was a village explainer – excellent if you were a village, but, if you were not, not.' Stein's notion of Pound has a certain callow justice – he was apt, in conversation as well as in print, to pronounce on anyone and anything in tones of rapt certainty. Malcolm Cowley has described him, in Paris, in just such a mood: '"I've found the lowdown on the Elizabethan drama!" he said . . . he was always finding the "lowdown", the inside story and the simple reason why.'

But by now Pound was trying to explain things to himself rather than to other people. By the summer of 1923 he had finished his revision of the opening *Cantos* and had sketched in what were to become the main contours of the work. William Bird had agreed to

Gertrude Stein. She was not a great admirer of Pound: perhaps he threatened her literary pre-eminence. She confessed that she 'did not find him amusing'.

publish *A Draft of XVI Cantos*, and Pound was ready now to go further. Although still troubled by doubts about the poem's obscurity, he believed his work to be the epic of the future, a poem combining history and himself in an apocalyptic statement of the way things 'really' are. His attitude to his contemporaries is significant in this respect. He had, for example, been praising *Ulysses* for five years but, in retrospect, he saw it in rather different terms: 'Mr Joyce's book was the END, it was the completion (literally speaking) of an era. It cooked up and served the unmitigated god damn stink of the decaying usury era.' The 'Pound Era', the era of the *Cantos*, was a new beginning; the work of his colleagues and contemporaries was out of date from the start.

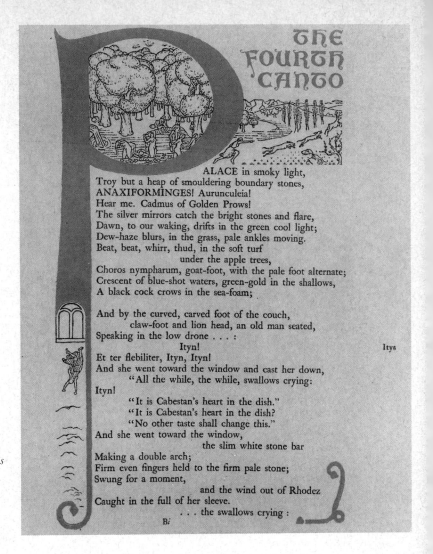

THE FOURTH CANTO

PALACE in smoky light,
Troy but a heap of smouldering boundary stones,
ANAXIFORMINGES! Aurunculeia!
Hear me. Cadmus of Golden Prows!
The silver mirrors catch the bright stones and flare,
Dawn, to our waking, drifts in the green cool light;
Dew-haze blurs, in the grass, pale ankles moving.
Beat, beat, whirr, thud, in the soft turf
                under the apple trees,
Choros nympharum, goat-foot, with the pale foot alternate;
Crescent of blue-shot waters, green-gold in the shallows,
A black cock crows in the sea-foam;

And by the curved, carved foot of the couch,
        claw-foot and lion head, an old man seated,
Speaking in the low drone . . . :
                Ityn!
Et ter flebiliter, Ityn, Ityn!   Itys
And she went toward the window and cast her down,
        "All the while, the while, swallows crying:
Ityn!
        "It is Cabestan's heart in the dish."
        "It is Cabestan's heart in the dish?
        "No other taste shall change this."
And she went toward the window,
                the slim white stone bar
Making a double arch;
Firm even fingers held to the firm pale stone;
Swung for a moment,
                and the wind out of Rhodez
Caught in the full of her sleeve.
                . . . the swallows crying :
        Bi

The opening of The Fourth Canto, from *A Draft of XVI Cantos* published by William Bird's Three Mountains Press in Paris, January 1925. The initials were designed by Henry Strater. 'He has wandered all over the page,' Pound complained to Bird.

Opposite: Pound in the courtyard of his Paris studio, 1923. 'He was much more in his element in Paris,' Wyndham Lewis wrote. 'I actually believe he cooked better in Paris than he did in London.'

For, despite his association with the leaders of cultural 'fashion', Pound never quite fitted in. Paris, too, 'demanded an image of its accelerated grimace' – as he had written in *Hugh Selwyn Mauberley* – and Pound was unwilling or unable to provide one. He was still too restless; his enthusiasm for Social Credit and for the wilder shores of politics lent him an ambiguous reputation among other Americans, and he was not interested enough in the work of younger French writers to acquire any kind of cult following. He had also been developing a bad temper. Eliot wrote to John Quinn during this period, 'It is harder to help Pound than anyone else. Apart from the fact that he is very sensitive and proud and that I have to keep an attitude of discipleship to him (as indeed I ought), every time I print anything of his it nearly sinks the paper [*The Egoist*].' In any case

Paris, as far as Pound was concerned, was becoming too self-conscious: 'There was, a bit later, so far as it came to the undersigned, the more glittering Paris, now everyman's Paris. Picabia gone to hell, Brancusi universally recognized by the cognoscenti, Cocteau in *Vogue* and finally Léger's photo in *Vanity Fair*.' Pound was restless now, sensing that he was in the right time but in the wrong place.

In fact Pound's last entrepreneurial effort was to help Ford Madox Ford launch his *Transatlantic Review* at the beginning of 1924. But by the autumn of that year he had had enough. He was in bad health; the new French writers – the Surrealist poets among them – were ignoring him; his poetry was still more admired than read. Paris, after all, had not turned out to be the city he either expected or wanted. He described the place, in *The Dial*, as 'an enervated centre'. He was thinking ahead to his new home and his new work; Paris and London, and the world which he had created around himself in both places, were finished. Now another place captured his imagination: Italy. In the October of 1924, the Pounds moved to Rapallo. Olga Rudge followed.

When Ezra and Dorothy Pound arrived in Rapallo, they were returning to a place which they knew well from previous visits. It could not have been more unlike their previous centres of residence, which is probably why Pound chose it: 'Rapallo', he wrote later, 'is a town officially of 15,000 inhabitants, 10,000 being peasants who live up on the hills.' It all seemed incomparably picturesque and, if Pound were to concentrate on his work at last, this was obviously the place in which to do it. But Pound was never to acquire the right degree of self-discipline, and the earnest concentration which he so longed for was never to be achieved. Rapallo, instead, became the setting for some of the most bizarre scenes of his life.

The Pounds spent their first few months in hotels, but eventually they found a small apartment in Via Marsala. It was on the fifth floor of the Albergo Rapallo, with a roof terrace which overlooked the Bay of Tigulio. Pound scattered around his home-made furniture and, at last, seemed to feel at home. His life as a professional American expatriate had always been one of ultimate refusal to 'blend' satisfactorily with the native fauna – he had needed, provoked, and then been embittered by, public comment and disapproval. But in Rapallo there seemed very little left to prove, and very few people to impress. The citizens accepted him readily enough, and he was soon known simply as *il poeta*; Gaudier-Brzeska's bust was in the window of the restaurant where he frequently ate, and Brigit Patmore, a friend of Pound's, remembers him in her memoir, *My Friends when Young*, in these early years 'sitting in a quiet café during the un-busy hours, playing chess with the waiters'. For a man who for thirty years had been dreaming of a civilized and humane Europe, this might have been the place finally to discover the reality.

For the next few years his work moved forward steadily; the *Cantos* were slowly being produced; his opera, *Le Testament*, was performed in

Opposite: Ford Madox Ford and Pound in Paris, *c.* 1923. It was during this period that the two men collaborated on the *Transatlantic Review*.

Rapallo - Panorama

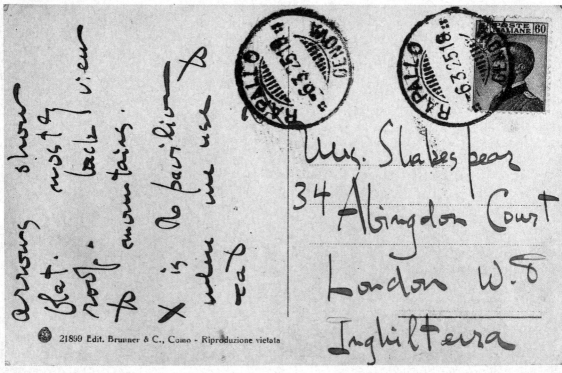

arrows show
that. mostq
rosy. back view
to mountains.
X is le pavilion
when we use
to eat

POSTE ITALIANE 60

RAPALLO GENOVA
-6.3.25 18

RAPALLO
-6.3.25 18

Mrs. Shakespear
34 Abingdon Court
London W.8
Inghilterra

21899 Edit. Brunner & C., Como - Riproduzione vietata

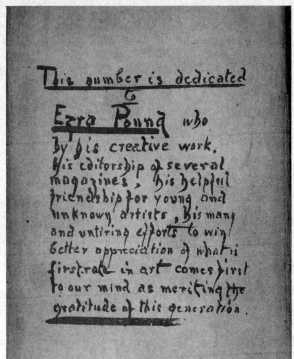

This number is dedicated to Ezra Pound who by his creative work, his editorship of several magazines, his helpful friendship for young and unknown artists, his many and untiring efforts to win better appreciation of what is firstrate in art comes first to our mind as meriting the gratitude of this generation.

Paris; and, in 1927, he started a periodical called *The Exile*. His political and intellectual interests were not yet as narrow or as obsessive as they were later to become and, for a man who was to turn into so convinced a Fascist, it is worth noting that even at this late date he had not actually chosen a course between rival ideologies: 'Both Fascio and the Russian revolution are interesting phenomena,' he wrote in *The Exile* of spring 1927.

Both, of course, were totalitarian in spirit – Pound was convinced of the need for some social system other than that of Western capitalism, for some alternative vision of human behaviour. He himself was estranged permanently from the old order: 'As I see things at present, I shall never again take any steps whatsoever to arrange publication of any of my work in either England or America.' This turned out to be no more than a characteristically rhetorical gesture, but it is at least a mark of Pound's increasing alienation. He was still promulgating his own idiosyncratic version of Social Credit, but his demand for other ways of seeing the world went further and deeper than this. He was now reading Confucius with great attention, and he was also studying the work of Leo Frobenius. Frobenius was a German historian whose notion of 'paideuma' – 'the tangle or complex of the inrooted ideas of any period', as Pound put it – was in direct contrast to the generalities of orthodox historians. All in all, Pound was seriously preparing himself to write an alternative history of the West.

Left: Ezra Pound, a photograph by Man Ray. 'He is better looking than in his youth,' a friend wrote, 'and obviously exceptionally healthy.'

Right: Dedication to Pound in the first issue of *This Quarter*, edited by Ernest Walsh and Ethel Moorhead. Miss Moorhead later withdrew the encomium: 'We take back our too generous dedication.'

Opposite: Postcard of Rapallo. Yeats described the bay as 'Rapallo's thin line of broken mother-of-pearl.'

M. et Mme Ezra Pound vous invitent à une audition privée

Paroles de Villon

Airs and fragments from an opéra

LE TESTAMENT

Texte de Villon   Musique par Ezra Pound

à la SALLE PLEYEL

22, Rue Rochechouart

Le Mardi soir

29 Juin 1926

(à 9 heures 15)

PROGRAMME

(probablement)

Hommage ou ouverture	cornet de dessus
Et mourut Paris	ténor et violon
Je plains	ténor et violon
Mort j'appelle	ténor et violon
Motif	
False beauté	ténor, violon et clavecin

Yves Tinayre, ténor — Olga Rudge, violon

Paul Tinayre

| Heaulmière | les mêmes |

Motifs de la foule, mélange violon, clavecin et cuivres

| Si J'ayme et sers | basse et cuivres |
| Frères Humains | ensemble |

Robert Maitland, basse — Yves Tinayre, ténor

Olga Rudge et Paul Tinayre, et cuivres

CLAVECIN PLEYEL

admet   personnes

On vous prie de présenter cette fiche

Salle Pleyel. 29 Juin, 9 h. 15 du soir E. P.

Invitation to the first performance of Pound's opera *Le Testament* on 29 June 1926. Cocteau, Eliot, Joyce and Hemingway, among others, were present.

But, still, in the Twenties, he was concerned with more conventional activities. In 1926, he travelled to Paris for the première of *Le Testament* at the Salle Pleyel (Cocteau, Joyce, Eliot and Hemingway were in the audience, and Virgil Thomson described it as perhaps 'the finest poet's music since Thomas Campion'), and of Antheil's *Ballet Mécanique*. But, apart from these isolated social appearances, he was steadily becoming more estranged from his friends. Joyce and he had become distant, and their friendship was not helped by Pound's decidedly negative reaction to *Finnegans Wake*. He wrote to Joyce in November 1926, 'Nothing short of divine vision or a new cure for the clapp can possibly be worth all the circumambient peripherization.' Despite the fact that Eliot had been, since 1925, an editor at Faber and Gwyer (later known as Faber and Faber), and was indirectly responsible for the publication of Pound's later books, he too played a less prominent role in Pound's life. He wrote afterwards, in *Poetry*, 'There did come a point, of course, at which difference of outlook and belief became too wide; or it may have been distance and different environment; or it may have been both.'

It was only with Yeats, in fact, that Pound maintained a steady friendship, though this may have been a result of their proximity. Yeats and his wife had visited Rapallo, liked it, and decided to stay. The two poets therefore saw a good deal of each other in the late Twenties. Yeats himself has left a memoir of their Italian friendship in *A Packet for Ezra Pound*, which includes an interesting discussion of the evolving *Cantos*, comparing the poem to a Bach fugue, and also provides a perceptive insight into Pound's own temperament in a description of his practice of feeding the stray cats of Rapallo: 'Yet, as I now recall the scene, I think he has no affection for cats . . .' It was simply that 'everybody speaks of them with contempt', and 'I examine his criticism in this new light, his praise of writers pursued by ill luck.' Many years later Pound was to inform Olson that he (Pound) belonged to 'the cat family'. By then, of course, everyone spoke of him also with something approaching contempt.

In this period, too, Pound's emotional life became immeasurably more complicated – but, characteristically, he worked hard to avoid any personal inconvenience. Olga Rudge and Pound were still lovers, and in July 1925 Miss Rudge gave birth to a daughter. The little girl, Maria, was quickly despatched to a peasant family in Bressanone in the Italian Tyrol. Money was put on the table; she was adopted, temporarily, at the cost of two hundred lire per month. Pound was later to take an active interest in her upbringing and education, but for the time being the infant was put to one side. Pound was adept in such matters; when Dorothy herself gave birth to their son Omar in Paris in 1926, the boy was immediately sent to London, to be raised by his maternal grandmother. Pound was to see him infrequently over the next twenty years. Meanwhile, in Italy, an arrangement had been concocted which suited Pound very well: Dorothy would spend the summers in England with her son, while Pound and Olga went to Venice. It was a neat solution, the neatness testifying to Pound's passion for organizing everything around him, but he never seems to have taken adequate account of the fact that such neatness might be at the expense of the lives of those who were closest to him – Dorothy, Olga, the children themselves.

There were further complications. His parents, too, had come to live in Rapallo – Homer Pound had retired from the Mint, and what could have been nicer than to be near the son whom they adored? Pound's reaction to his parents' decision is not known, but they settled in comfortably enough. Homer, the genial and extrovert Westerner, was liked by the villagers; Isabel was more prickly and aloof – she appreciated cultural conversation, and was in the habit of reciting Pound's juvenilia (the poetry written, of course, when he had been living with her) in public.

A PACKET FOR EZRA POUND:
BY WILLIAM BUTLER YEATS.

THE CUALA PRESS
DUBLIN, IRELAND
MCMXXVIV

Title page of W. B. Yeats's memoir of Pound. Yeats completed the book at Rapallo. He had written to Olivia Shakespear of his neighbours: 'Ezra and Dorothy seem happy and content, pleased with their way of life.'

Right: Homer Pound, Ezra Pound and Ezra's daughter by Olga Rudge, Maria, in 1929. In her memoir, *Discretions*, Maria commented: 'Over the chaos hovers one certainty. I, the child, was wanted. The rest is music and poetry.'

Below: Portrait of Omar Pound, Pound's son, by e. e. cummings. Omar was born in September 1926, and this was sketched on 19 August 1948.

Pound himself now thought continually of the work at hand, and of the poetry to come. Throughout the Twenties he composed the *Cantos* and, just before Homer Pound left for Italy, Pound had written to his father about the eventual shape of the poem: 'Rather like, or unlike subject and response and counter subject in fugue. A.A. Live man goes down into world of Dead. C.B. The "repeat in history". B.C. The "magic moment" or moment of metamorphosis . . .' But Yeats, while accepting the author's analogy with the movement of a fugue, had also said, in *A Packet for Ezra Pound*, 'He is not trying to create forms because he believes, like so many of his contemporaries, that old forms are dead, so much as a new style, a new man . . .' Formal or formless? It is not clear if Pound himself knew, and succeeding volumes of the *Cantos* were simply entitled 'Drafts'. *A Draft of XVI Cantos* appeared in 1925; *A Draft of Cantos XVII–XXVII* was

from a # cont. nued

+ then went down to ship.

    set keel to ~~sea~~ *breakers*

for + on the godly sea ~

We set up mast, + sail,

    on the swarty ship. ,

Sleep bore us aboard her ,

    + our bodies also

heavy will weeping.

    + winds from sternward

bore our out onward, with

    bellying ~ canvass

Manuscript of the opening to Canto I, originally planned as the opening of Canto III. Certain changes have been made in the final, published version.

published in 1928; and, in 1930, the Hours Press in Paris printed *A Draft of XXX Cantos.*

The main contours of the poem were now evident; A *Draft of XXX Cantos* opens with a mythical descent into the realm of the dead, and closes with the specific, mundane death of Pope Alessandro Borgia. Although this poetry is visionary in intent, with the clarity of a transcendental beauty pushed against a false or conventional reality, it is epic in method. By including historical detail and the harmonies of orthodox lyric, together with autobiographical reminiscences, satire and passages of meditation, Pound is attempting to provide a composite portrait of his age – a novel and uncompromising portrait which would shock the readers of the *Cantos* into an awareness of the disturbed and complex world around them. It can easily be forgotten how revolutionary Pound's poetic style was at the time: in 1930, he was writing a poetry which included extensive prose quotations – even transcribed letters – as an integral part of its movement.

But the *Cantos*' loose structure is the only one which could encompass the breadth and wealth of detail which Pound insisted on commanding; meditations on the gods jostle against urban ironies, Eleanor of Aquitaine can be placed beside a dissertation on usury. Everything which is significant is still contemporaneous, and Pound was trying to recreate what he described in an essay on Cavalcanti as 'a radiant world where one thought cuts through another with clean edge, a world of moving energies'. Pound's heroic tone was designed to keep together these disparate and energetic elements; it was his sense – transmitted through the rhythmic confidence of his lines – that poetry can lay claim to the whole world, that nothing is beyond its range. His days of Provençal romance and Parisian irony were now finally buried; to bring together the transcendental and the actual, to see the light moving between them, it was necessary for him to range over the whole of the world's history. Nothing, in this epic of the word, could be lost. This conception of the poem's role means that it sometimes veers perilously close to rhetoric; the lines sometimes crack, become broken and discontinuous, under the strain of Pound's grand intentions. But at its best the poem combines the actual and the lyrical in ways that suggest a fresh extension of the imaginative impulse, and of the possibilities of poetic statement:

> And Tovarisch lay in the wind
> And the sun lay over the wind,
> And three forms became in the air
> And hovered about him,
>   so that he said:
> This machinery is very ancient,
>   surely we have heard this before.

But the *Cantos*, although they expressed his passionate hatred of social and economic corruption, were not enough in themselves to satisfy Pound's increasingly obsessive concern with the financial and political systems of the West; in addition, his sense of estrangement in Italy – he was becoming known to some of his friends as the 'Rapallo troglodyte' – was turning into a feeling of rejection. He wrote to the American editor, Louis Untermeyer, in 1930: 'P. was able to state that NO american pubshr. had *ever* accepted a book on his recommendation! no am. univ. or cultural institution had ever invited him to lecture . . .' When he felt thus threatened he tended to attack – but in increasingly unpredictable ways. Contemporary accounts of Pound in the Thirties tend to dwell upon the strange disparities which were now emerging in his behaviour. On the one hand he was more relaxed, and looked healthier, than in Paris or London: he swam, he played tennis, he liked to tell jokes, he was a good mimic. During this period, too, he was busy creating a miniature artistic community: from 1933 he and Olga Rudge organized a series of concerts in Rapallo's town hall, where a wide range of music, including that of

Bartók and Vivaldi, was played and analysed. 'The Rapallo concerts have provided a laboratory for the objective study of music,' Pound wrote in 1936. But there was another, less pleasant, aspect of his character; he was given to what one biographer has called attacks of 'exaggerated belligerency'. Yeats had already remarked, according to Richard Aldington, 'how mysterious it was that a man who was "so distinguished" in most of his poems except *Lustra* should in real life often be so uncouth, so jarring.' Joyce was said by now to have grown frightened of being alone with him. A chance remark would leave Pound speechless. His daughter Maria remembers him in such a mood, 'visibly fighting a wasp nest in his brain'. He was becoming manic, tending to lecture perfect strangers, not listening to what they had to say in reply, interested only in talking about his own preoccupations – the nature of money and, increasingly, the nature of Fascism.

He had started to date his letters by the Fascist calendar in 1931, and in 1933 he was granted a brief audience with Benito Mussolini, whose assertion that 'poetry is a necessity to the State' had particularly won Pound's approval. He presented the dictator with his proposals for monetary reform, together with a copy of *A Draft of XXX Cantos*; Mussolini was graciously pleased to call the work '*divertente*'. 'Don't knock Mussolini,' Pound had earlier written to a friend. 'He will end up with Sigismundo and the men of order . . . I believe that anything human will and understanding of contemporary Italy cd. accomplish, he has done and will continue to do.'

Pound's commitment to Fascism is not easy to explain. The 'revolutionary simpleton', as Wyndham Lewis called him, had always been attached to the idea of an élitist European 'order', and Fascism seemed to promise that. Right-wing, anti-democratic regimes often pay lip-service to the kind of 'high' imaginative culture which Pound himself espoused. In addition, Mussolini's economic programme seemed, at first glance (which was all Pound gave it), closer to the notions of Social Credit than anyone else's. But, more importantly, Pound's temperament was an obsessive one – he loved order, he organized everyone and everything, he was impatient with anything other than neat and speedy solutions: Fascism offered them. He had formed groups and gangs during his days of literary propagandizing, and there was no reason why he should not embrace a similar totalitarianism in his political activities. And, under pressure, his paranoia grew: the Western system of publishers and editors was oppressing him, he was starved both of readers and of funds, there were always people rising up to strike him. He needed a scapegoat, and his rootless anger fell upon the Jews. His wrath – like his affection – was curiously impersonal. He got on very well with individual Jews (like the American poet, Louis Zukofsky, whom he championed), and the Rapallo concerts had Jewish performers even after the introduction of the race laws in Italy; but he detested 'the Jew' and 'the kike' in the abstract. His paranoia was the same as that which, in more powerful and determined men, led to the construction of Auschwitz

JEFFERSON
AND/OR
MUSSOLINI

L'IDEA STATALE
FASCISM AS I HAVE SEEN IT

BY

EZRA POUND
Volitionist Economics

NEW YORK: LIVERIGHT PUBLISHING CORP.
LONDON: STANLEY NOTT

Title page to the first edition of *Jefferson and/or Mussolini*. 'No typescript of mine', Pound wrote in his foreword, 'has been read by so many people or brought me a more interesting correspondence.'

and Dachau. Pound directly implicated himself, through his writings, in the horrors of Fascism.

For although his work as a poet was mediated by a refined and harmonious language (history itself, in the *Cantos*, anchors Pound's genius), there was no such resourcefulness in his other, more immediate, writings. He was to become a voracious propagandist. By the mid-Thirties, he was writing literally thousands of letters – to bankers, politicians, academics, monetary reform groups – often of the most belligerent and incoherent kind. His study in Rapallo was strung with ropes, from which dangled the documents and articles which Pound might need to quote. He wrote article after article, for any magazine in practically any country – in 1935, for example, he was responsible for some 150 contributions to periodicals. His enthusiasms were now uncontrollable; when his daughter introduced him to young Italians with literary aspirations, he 'would immediately challenge the newcomer by pulling out a ten-lira note and telling him to look at it carefully. What did it mean? . . . Until he understood the nature of money, he could not understand or write good poetry.' His letters became steadily more eccentric, many of them couched in a private slang which it is difficult to follow.

For all his attempts to keep at the centre of events, in fact, he had retreated into a private world of fantasy from which he never fully escaped. His role as a 'village explainer' had a certain authenticity when it came to the appreciation of literature, since his instinctively good ear prevented him from making crucial mistakes. 'The simple reason why' works when there is judgment of genius behind it. But Pound's attempts to transfer the same modes of judgment from literature to political and economic matters were quite inadequate. He assumed that human beings, like words, could be easily freed from 'emotional slither'; he scrutinized Western economies as though they were poetic texts, for which a close reading would provide the solution. People as such never really existed for him – Wyndham Lewis had said, with some justice, that Pound 'never seems to have *seen* the individual at all' – but a politics without people is both wilful and inappropriate. 'A thousand candles together blaze with intense brightness,' he wrote in *A Visiting Card* (1942), 'No one candle's light damages another's. So is the liberty of the individual in the ideal and Fascist state.' This is a pleasing aesthetic image, but politics and economics are not subdivisions of aesthetics – this was Pound's central error and, when compounded with paranoia, it could lead only to disaster. He had lost touch with the world, and the world would eventually fall upon him.

By the end of the Thirties, his articles and letters were beginning to bore or to anger even his closest friends. And when Pound travelled to the United States in 1939, 'to keep hell from breaking loose in the world', as he was to say later, he was not a success. He lectured those few Senators who agreed to see him, picked arguments with academics, and alienated his friends. William Carlos Williams wrote, after Pound's visit, to James Laughlin (the publisher of *New Directions*

The 1939 Commencement at Hamilton College, where Pound received an honorary degree. Pound used the occasion to attack the anti-Fascist opinions of the man in the middle, H. V. Kaltenborn, a journalist.

The cover of Pound's *How To Read*, published in December 1931. The purpose of the book was not to muddle the student 'by making him read more books, but to allow him to read fewer with greater results'.

and one of Pound's old friends): 'The man is sunk, in my opinion, unless he can shake the fog of Fascism out of his brain during the next few years.' Pound himself was aware of the impression he was creating. 'I don't want to roast little babies,' he said rather defensively to Virginia Rice, an American literary agent who had 'placed' some of his work. 'I just happen to like the Fascist money system.' But even the most sympathetic observers now realized that something was badly wrong; after his return to Italy from the United States Pound met the philosopher George Santayana, and he was, according to Santayana, 'full of scraps of culture but lost, lost, lost in the intellectual world.'

Yet it is an odd fact in Pound's career that he achieved some of his best – his most mature and coherent – work at the time he was most disturbed by his political and economic obsessions. Some of his finest critical writing – *Make It New*, *ABC of Reading*, *Guide to Kulchur*, *Polite Essays* for example – appeared in the Thirties. Of course, the books are occasionally marked by inconsequence or overemphasis – Pound's prose style is harsh, didactic, restless, moving quickly from point to point – but as a body of sustained critical writing they are both cogent and persuasive.

In *ABC of Reading* (published 1943), for example, the notion of literature as a force 'to promote clarity and vigour' is not an original one, but it is reaffirmed with a lucidity and forcefulness that still command assent: 'Literature', as Pound put it, 'is news that STAYS news.' Although the reader may cavil at Pound's choice of the 'significant' writers – his taste is sometimes wilfully arcane – his

HOW TO READ BY EZRA POUND

commitment to the renewal and renovation of language gives his writing an edge which other, more cautious, criticism lacks. He treated literature as a form of scientific enquiry, with certain specimens to be examined and certain 'discoveries' which remain true and exact. Pound is able to cut through obfuscating generalities and academic cant with a disciplined attention to the actual texts (no critic has ever quoted so much good work or, it must be admitted, at such length), and to what he saw to be of permanent value: 'The critic is either a parasite, or he is concerned with the growth of the next paideuma.'

This 'paideuma', the body of ideas and artefacts that forms a culture, can only be understood fitfully and obliquely by those who are part of it. It was for this reason that Pound, in *Guide to Kulchur*, experiments with the obliquity of his 'ideogrammic method', in which 'gists and piths' of learning or information are placed beside each other in a mutually revelatory process. He can move, within the space of three pages, from Japanese poetry to English labourers to Italian text-books; this is no doubt a suitable way for Pound to deal with his inconsistent and sometimes incoherent theorizing but, despite the *longueurs* and the false trails, the thread of his concerns remains clear. Language is the conscience of the race; it must retain its sharpness and its clarity, otherwise civilization itself will become slack and disingenuous. His concern is with the actual rather than the general, with a culture and a vocabulary that rest upon perceived facts and genuine values.

It is this sense which runs, too, through Pound's economic writings published in the same decade: *ABC of Economics*, *Child's Guide to Economics*, *Social Credit: an Impact*. Although these texts were also written during one of the high periods of Pound's 'literary' activity, his central point was that the active world could not be segregated into such categories as 'literature', 'economics' and 'history'. Just as economic conditions 'become increasingly capable of forcing the degradation of books', so capitalism itself is degraded because it 'has set NO value whatsoever on fine perceptions or on literary capacity'. 'Kulchur' comprises an intricate series of facts, perceptions and artefacts which are massively interrelated; bad government and a corrupt language tend to disguise the truth of this totality by concentrating upon what is conventional or meretricious. The secret is to see the 'kulchur' whole by discarding orthodox habits of thought: 'It does not matter a two-penny damn whether you load up your memory with the chronological sequence of what has happened . . . so long as you understand the process now going on, or the processes biological, social, economic now going on, enveloping you as an individual, in a social order.'

This sense of 'the process', of human history as something which can be readily understood by the application of a 'few very simple principles', also informs the method of the *Cantos* during this period. Having sketched out the canvas in the first thirty sections, Pound now used the techniques and insights thus gained in order to reconstruct

Dorothy Shakespear's designs for the initials of the *Cantos*; they were never published. The Second World War, unfortunately, intervened.

and interpret the pattern of world events: 'The enemy', he was to say later, 'is the suppression of history.' The *Cantos*, then, represent the return of the suppressed. He had already explained in *Guide to Kulchur* that 'there is no mystery about the *Cantos*, they are the tale of the tribe'. And, complementing this radical humanist endeavour, he wrote to a correspondent, 'I don't expect in the end to have introduced ethical novelties or notions, though I hope to light up a few ancient bases.' *Eleven New Cantos* (31–41, published in 1934) interpret modern history, largely through the examples of Jefferson and Quincy Adams – but also through the exemplary use of satire and lyric. *The Fifth Decad of Cantos* (42–51, published in 1937) documents the history of usury – the enemy, as Pound saw it, of human growth and natural fertility – and the hopeless struggle against it. *Cantos LII–LXXI*, published in 1940, deal with Chinese history and with the career of John Adams, both illustrating the proper and harmonious conduct of a nation by righteous leaders. This summary of the succeeding volumes necessarily provides only the most basic description, since other elements and other kinds of discourse are continually being introduced by Pound. The wealth of detail and the constant shifting of themes and contexts defy any but the most elaborate analysis; it should be noted, though, that the more perceptive critics of the *Cantos* see them as embodying and illustrating a series of contrasts: natural abundance as opposed to artificial scarcity, linear clock-time in contrast to transcendental moments of vision, and so on.

But the *Cantos* raise other, and more general, literary problems. Pound's attempt to introduce political and economic concerns into a primarily 'poetic' context has been criticized on the grounds that it is both boring and simplistic. But the attempt, in the *Cantos*, to create a language of social debate within an unfamiliar moral and literary context, is interesting, and, in the light of the prevailing mediocrity of political dialogue, Pound's effort to clarify and deepen such debate is not an unworthy one. Sometimes the writing is too obscure or only sporadically interesting; under the pressure of Pound's attempts to be rigorous and 'objective', it breaks apart. But, clearly, the *Cantos* represent a unique way of dealing with contemporary history and the historical past; only if our definition of what is 'poetic', and what is not, is a narrow one do such matters seem irrelevant or unnecessary. The *Cantos* represent Pound's attempt to encompass the whole range of human activity; and his perception of the 'paideuma' – of cultural unity – was an insistent one. He saw no contradiction between lyric and polemic, between monetary reform and visionary harmonies. His work is inevitably obscure if we do not understand why he is doing it; and the *Cantos* are difficult only if we go to them with conventional expectations about the nature of poetry.

Pound's contemporaries, however, would not have agreed with this assessment. Joyce, Lewis and Eliot were all unhappy with Pound's project and, although there had been a revival of interest in his work in the early Thirties (largely engineered by Eliot), the later *Cantos* were, predictably, received with hostility or bemusement. Even Yeats wrote of Pound's poetry, in his introduction to the *Oxford Book of Modern Verse*, 'It is constantly interrupted, broken, twisted into nothing by . . . nervous obsession, nightmare, stammering confusion.' At its most rhetorical, Pound's work is indeed broken and disorganized, but the general structure of the work is not so; Pound himself described his method as one designed for the eye and the ear just as much as for the mind: 'Abbreviations save eye effort . . . ALL typographical disposition, placing of words on the page, is intended to facilitate the reader's intonation. There is no *intentional* obscurity.'

In fact the disconnectedness of much of Pound's poetry – the moving from point to point, line to discontinuous line, which seemed to Yeats to be a register of 'stammering confusion' – is actually a deliberate technique to exert the maximum strength from the words on the page. It is a transcript of the workings of the possessed imagination – direct, unmediated by orthodox syntax or rhetorical glissades. The conjunction of lyric and polemic, prose and ideogram, means that each element derives a kind of extra-curricular strength from its location in such an unfamiliar context. The political edge to Pound's writing gives a unique resourcefulness to his lyric passages, and his polemical discourse derives its connotative value from the passages of lyric beauty which surround it. The faults which clearly do exist in the poem tend to be, as Pound said of Bartók's music, 'the defects inherent in a record of struggle'.

It was only in his poetry, however, that he was able to resolve such struggles. He was never able to transpose the same discipline into his own life, or into those prejudices which bubbled up from below the surface of his psyche and burst into the air. He had never really taken the trouble, or been able, to find out what kind of person he was – hence his continual playing of roles – and by 1940 too much had been done and said for him to be able to retain his stability. During the early years of the Second World War he contributed articles of a rabidly anti-Semitic kind to Japanese and Italian magazines. During these years he wrote only two Cantos, LXXII and LXXIII; they are both in Italian, have never been published, but concern in part the

heroic struggle of the German-Italian resistance behind Allied lines. As Maria, his daughter, put it: 'He was losing ground, I now see, losing grip on what most specifically he should have been able to control: his own words . . .'

These were years of terrible insecurity; by the end of 1941, Pound was an American citizen living in and off a country at war with his native land. After Pearl Harbor, Pound tried to return home but an American Embassy official turned down his application – for reasons that are still mysterious. And so the Pounds, with Homer and Isabel, and with Olga, stayed on. Pound, being the sole provider, was considerably overworked. In fact most of his earnings came only in small amounts from his broadcasts for Rome Radio.

These broadcasts were to prove his undoing. He struck a prophetic note in a letter he wrote to the English poet, Ronald Duncan, in 1940: 'Blasted friends left a goddam radio here yester. Gift. God damn destructive and dispersive devil of an invention. But got to be faced . . .' However, despite the misgivings of some Italian bureaucrats, who considered the strange American poet to be a 'pleasant enough madman', Pound began to broadcast for the Italian government in January 1941 and continued to do so until July 1943. He talked for seven minutes, during the 'American hour', ten times each month; he received approximately seventeen dollars for each session.

These broadcasts were the culmination of his role as a rebel and outsider; he had long been used to his ideas being treated with contempt, and nothing could now stop him from saying exactly what he meant. In a variety of theatrical voices, from the folksy drawl of a Midwestern American to the clipped tones of a Confucian 'sage', Pound – often introduced in a preamble as 'the professor' or 'the well-known poet

Pound, 1939, preliminary sketch and finished portrait by Wyndham Lewis. 'A true, disinterested and unspoilt individual,' Lewis had called him. Pound visited Lewis's studio in Notting Hill Gate for a number of sittings. When Lewis asked his advice about the composition of the painting Pound replied: 'Ef you must diddle an MONKEY with problumbs you take a GNU canvasss or paper and you do a ABStrakk dEEsign.'

and economist' – delivered himself of his opinions. His tone is generally that of an exasperated schoolmaster, talking to 'you kids': 'I dislike quoting Jewish scripture. But the crop comes from the seed. By Jews you have betrayed a number of nations. And by the Jews you will, I think, in your turn be betrayed . . . the kike is all out for power. The kike and the unmitigated evil that is centred in London . . . And every sane act you commit is committed in homage to Mussolini and Hitler . . . You are at war for the duration of the Germans' pleasure . . . I lose my thread at times, so much that I can't count on anyone's mind.'

The broadcasts are sometimes concerned with literary and cultural statements which are both perceptive and amusing. But the general effect of reading the transcripts is devastating: rambling, Jew-baiting, self-deluded, often sickeningly brutal. As a result Pound was indicted in 1943, in the United States, for treason. When he heard the news, he wrote from Rapallo to the Attorney-General in Washington: 'I do not feel that the simple fact of speaking over the radio, wherever placed, can in itself constitute treason.' But he was by now very tired, in despair at the sudden collapse of Mussolini, and resigned to whatever form his eventual fate might take. His personal life, also, was not without its own suffering.

His father had died in Rapallo in 1942, and in the following year the Germans insisted, for their own safety, that the Pounds vacate their flat by the seafront. So Dorothy and Ezra moved in with Olga Rudge, who was living up the hill in Sant'Ambrogio. The two women were forced together: hatred and distrust filled the house. Pound was reaping the fruits of what he had sown so long ago, just as the scatterings of his Fascism and anti-Semitism were soon to bear a bitter harvest. His daughter has testified to the fact, however, that Pound was quite without self-pity during this period. One of his 'laws for Maria', when she was a small child, had been 'that if she suffers, it is her own fault for not understanding the universe. That so far as her father knows suffering exists in order to make people think.' But events were now moving too fast for ordinary thought. In September 1942, the Allies prepared to invade Italy.

Pound was in Rome at the time, and the city was in chaos. His only way out was on foot and, eventually, by train. He travelled to Gais in the Tyrol, where his daughter was staying with the foster-mother upon whom he had dumped her many years before: 'I gave him water to wash with,' Maria wrote in her memoir *Discretions*, 'he was all covered with dust, like a beggar.' Pound told Maria, for the first time, of Dorothy and of his son, Omar: 'I felt no resentment,' Maria wrote, 'only a vague sense of pity.'

Pound then returned to Sant'Ambrogio and, as the Allies made their way toward him, kept on writing articles and pamphlets. No words of his, however, could now change his destiny. At the end of April, 1945, two Italian partisans came to the house and arrested him; a few days later, he was in Genoa in the care of the American military authorities. Here he declared to a journalist that Hitler was a martyr, and compared him with Joan of Arc. On 22 May, after interrogation, Pound was transferred to the American Disciplinary Training Center at Pisa: 'Exercise utmost security measures', the escorts were ordered, 'to prevent escape or suicide.' Pound arrived at Pisa on 24 May.

The camp at Pisa had been built to contain the most vicious or the most renegade military prisoners; it consisted of a barbed-wire stockade, with fourteen guard towers around the perimeter, altogether one half mile square in area. When Pound arrived, it held approximately 3,600 prisoners who were subjected to a routine both harsh and unremitting; any prisoner who tried to escape was shot on sight. A specially reinforced cage – ten feet square and seven feet high – was built to contain Pound, and at night he slept on its concrete floor. He was later to call it 'the gorilla cage'. One account, printed in *Esquire* magazine, gives a graphic report of his situation: 'He wore an Army fatigue uniform, unbuttoned at the neck. He walked back and forth on the concrete floor, making no effort to look outside. His trousers hung loose and his shoes were unlaced. A special guard stood outside his cage which, at night, was brilliantly lighted. Everyone looked at him.' The dust and the light soon became intolerable; he became physically very weak; he lost his memory; eventually, he broke down.

Pound was then transferred to the medical compound, where he was allowed to live in a small tent. Maria Rudge visited him here and reported that 'he had aged a lot and his eyes were inflamed'. But 'he had kept his trait of being most appreciative of small kindnesses.' Such kindnesses now included books – among them Legge's edition of Confucius – and the use of a typewriter. Despite his extraordinary predicament, Pound's native spirit soon returned; he wrote, from Pisa, to the English law firm of Shakespear and Parkyn: 'My most complete fog, my difficulty is my ABSOLUTE ignorance of what had happened in the USA and in England from 1940 to 1945 . . . The public has learned a great deal, but it still has the right to know more . . . Can you ask Mr Eliot whether Faber will be ready to print another volume of Cantos?'

These new Cantos were now being written in the medical compound, as Pound reflected upon the destiny which had delivered him there. He had written, three years earlier, 'We find two moments in history; one that divides, shatters and kills, and one that contemplates the unity of the mystery.' In this shattering moment, Pound was searching for the unity. In a sense all the *Cantos* had provided a context and a meaning for his scattered reading and his sometimes eccentric perceptions – the poem was the matrix of his life, giving strength and solidity to what would otherwise be stray and random notions (the form itself, both open and structured, perfectly suited the paradoxical temperament of the man). The *Cantos* were, quite literally, the means by which Pound saved himself.

The *Pisan Cantos* (74–84) are filled with this sense of loss redeemed – of old hopes abandoned, and failure understood. Pound composed

The Disciplinary Training Center, Pisa. In the centre are the death cells, and to the right is one of the segregation areas. The American army magazine, *Yank*, called it 'the toughest training detail in the Army . . . tougher even than front-line combat'.

The holding cells at Pisa. Pound's cage, specially reinforced with air-strip steel, is just visible on the left: 'No man who has passed a month in the death cells believes in cages for beasts.' (*Pisan Cantos*)

Pound working on the *Cantos* in the medical compound of Pisa. Here he also wrote letters for other prisoners, and typed out the final versions of *The Unwobbling Pivot* and *The Great Digest*. Chinese characters can be seen in the book open at his right hand.

Opposite: Jacket of the *Pisan Cantos*, published by New Directions in 1948. The book became the subject of scandal when it was awarded the Bollingen Prize for Poetry.

them on an old typewriter he had borrowed: 'The constant clanging and banging of the typewriter, which he punched always with his index fingers, were always accompanied by a high-pitched humming sound,' an observer in the medical compound wrote. Parcels of his hand-corrected scripts were then sent to Dorothy, now back in Rapallo, who in turn sent them on to Maria Rudge for retyping. But first they had to get past the base censor, and it was to placate him that Pound wrote one of the few coherent accounts of his own work:

The Cantos contain nothing in the nature of cypher or intended obscurity . . . There is also extreme condensation in the quotations, for example 'Mine eyes have' (given as mi-hine eyes hev) refers to the Battle Hymn of the Republic as heard from the loud-speaker . . . citations from Homer or Sophocles or Confucius are brief, and serve to remind the ready reader that we were not born yesterday . . . The form of the poem and the main progress is conditioned by its own inner shape, but the life of the DTC passing OUTSIDE the scheme cannot but impinge, or break into the main flow.

THE PISAN CANTOS OF EZRA POUND

And so the poem, although established in the real world now surrounding Pound (a world so real, so pressing, that it takes on an hallucinatory quality), also assumes its proper role as an historical and imaginative record. Events of the recent past had, however, destroyed Pound's fantasies about himself; now he was left with the smallest phenomena, which could not be faked, with their own bright life:

> and there was a smell of mint under the tent flaps
> especially after the rain . . .

and with recollections of his earlier time in England and in France. In the *Pisan Cantos* Pound reverts continually to his last years in London, as though trying to find a clue to the mystery: when did everything go wrong? The poetry here, despite its high critical reputation, is for this reason often self-indulgent. Although he is at the centre of the sequence for obvious reasons, Pound is often too commanding a figure:

> As a lone ant from a broken ant-hill
> from the wreckage of Europe, ego scriptor,

and the wanderings of his subjectivity often become obscure or disharmonious. The problem of poetic obscurity has in fact to be faced continually in the work, since Pound places it squarely at the centre of his poetry. But there are different forms of obscurity; in much of Pound's work it is of a fruitful and indeed necessary kind, since the lines reveal on further, puzzled examination certain internal parallels and patterns of resonance which are missed on a first reading. But in the *Pisan Cantos* the obscurity is often portentous and clumsy: madness, at least Pound's madness, is saying what he means without reference to any other context, whether social or linguistic. In this sequence Pound saves himself from self-reflective inanition only in the passages of intense observation, or in conventional lyric. But the rest of the poetry emerges as the rumblings of a wounded soul, a work of memory – or rather of nostalgia, the ghost of memory.

His balance had, indeed, momentarily deserted him under the pressure of events. On 16 November he was taken from Pisa, travelled to Rome, and was flown to Washington. By 18 November he was in a Washington jail. Here his lawyer, Julien Cornell, went to see him: 'I found the poor devil in a rather desperate condition,' he wrote to James Laughlin, 'He is very wobbly in his mind and while his talk is entirely rational, he flits from one idea to another and is unable to concentrate even to the extent of answering a single question.' On 25 November he had a temporary breakdown. 'When I asked him whether he wanted to stand mute or would prefer to enter a plea,' Cornell wrote later, 'he was unable to answer me. His mouth opened once or twice as if to speak, but no words came out. He looked up at the ceiling and his face began to twitch.' Pound was later vividly to describe, to D. D. Paige, the editor of Pound's selected correspondence, how he felt during this period of incarceration: 'He said that it seemed as though a movie film were running through his head and that suddenly the film would jam and break, and then there would be only a white light.'

On 27 November, Cornell made a formal request that Pound be transferred to a hospital. He testified in his affidavit that 'he was at once beset with fears – that he would be thrown with murderers and felons who would kill him'. Pound was in court when Cornell entered his plea, and Charles Olson watched him 'removing his glasses and rubbing his eyes, slumping in his chair and then leaning on the table, twisting for comfort, always working his hands.' On 4 December Pound was transferred to Gallinger Hospital, where he was examined by four psychiatrists. He had never cared for psychoanalysis, or its practitioners, and despite his ill-health he may have put on something of a performance for the benefit of his mental inquisitors: 'He insists', they wrote to Chief Justice Bolitha J. Laws, who was handling Pound's case, 'that his broadcasts were not treasonable, but that all his radio activities have stemmed from his self-appointed mission to "save the Constitution". He is abnormally grandiose, is expansive and exuberant in manner, exhibiting pressure of speech, discursiveness and distractability.' He had not, in fact, changed very much at all.

But he was judged insane, nevertheless, and on 21 December he was sent to a mental hospital, St Elizabeth's – to Howard Hall, its ward for the criminally insane. The conditions here were appalling; the ward reeked of sweat and urine; Pound called it 'the hell-hole'. And although he wrote, 'I remember a moment of quite irrational happiness in the hell-hole,' his general condition was one of considerable anxiety and unhappiness. He spoke to one psychiatrist 'of his mental processes being in a fog . . . a feeling of hollowness, going through this gesture with his fingers, describing the vortex of the skull.' He scribbled a letter to Cornell:

> grey mist barrier impassible
>   ignorance absolute
>   anonyme
>   futility of might have been
>   coherent areas
>   constantly
>   invaded
>   aiuto.

Aiuto is the Italian word for 'help'.

Charles Olson was one of Pound's first visitors (Laughlin had written to him, 'Go around and see him . . . he can't seem to concentrate on reading or writing, but he does enjoy talking to people – it seems to release some of his woes'), and has left the most detailed account of the poet's situation, in *Charles Olson & Ezra Pound. An Encounter at St Elizabeth's*, edited by Catherine Seelye. When Olson saw Pound, he had no possessions, he was worried about his family and frightened of other patients in Howard Hall: ' "There's an Indian in my ward who talks all the time about killing people." But then he said, quite quietly, that he didn't think there was anything wrong with him.' Olson adds here that 'it is the blindness which is the remaining sense, over-concentrated, obsessional, rushing ahead of the reality . . .' But Pound was still coherent, correcting friends over dates, lucid about his condition: 'If I had only read Confucius earlier,' he said to Olson on a later visit, 'I would not be in this mess.' The psychiatrists would not let him alone: 'He says Kavka keeps pounding questions at him . . . and punched his fist against the wall of his other hand to illustrate the effect.' There were, however, some poignant moments in their conversation: 'I said, "You make Gaudier seem so young" – and I went on with what I have thought so often, "as you seem to me yourself, so young." And he crushes his head and face in his hands, and says nothing.' But Pound's charm and wit often returned, even in those most dreadful of circumstances: 'I do not know anyone who could be in prison and stay as he.'

On 13 February a formal hearing was held to determine the extent of Pound's insanity, and the same four psychiatrists testified in front of a jury. As a result of their evidence, Pound was found to be of 'unsound mind' and once more confined to Howard Hall. He had escaped the death penalty for treason, but the rigours of imprisonment were only just beginning.

Dorothy Pound was eventually able to see her husband in July 1946: 'I have now seen Ezra three times,' she wrote to Cornell; 'I find him very nervous and jumpy. I believe his wits are really very scattered, and he has difficulty in concentrating for more than a few minutes.' But in 1947, after an application for bail had been turned down, Pound was moved to a more agreeable section of St Elizabeth's, the Chestnut Ward. Here he was to spend the next eleven years of his life.

St Elizabeth's is a very large hospital, in those days rambling over an area of some four hundred acres and holding approximately seven thousand patients. Pound, however, was something of a rarity among them; he tended to be supercilious with the other patients, obstreperous with his doctors ('One didn't have a mutual dialogue with him – he was at you,' one psychiatrist wrote afterwards), and steadfastly refused treatment. He played no part in the hospital's activities: instead, he turned himself into an island. He had been given a small alcove off one of the wards, shielded by a curtain, and it was here that he met and talked to his visitors. David Rattray, a journalist who visited Pound some years after his first confinement, has left a precise description of him under these extraordinary circumstances: the hall off which Pound entertained was 'very wide and dark as a subway station'. The alcove itself was shadowy, and the noises of television and radio blared continually. But Pound, apparently unmoved by these conditions, 'was everywhere at once, in a frenzy of activity, loading himself with jars of various sizes'. He was still excessively nervous, as ill at ease as ever, jumping up to type names and addresses for Rattray, still with his blustering manner: 'Well, I've been trying to make some people wake up to a number of simple facts, and they'd better hurry up, if they don't want to wake up too late to *do* anything.'

Opposite: Letter from Ezra Pound to his lawyer, Julien Cornell, from St Elizabeth's. It is dated January 1946. The 'Olson' referred to is Charles Olson, the American poet who visited Pound at St Elizabeth's.

Wednes. night
S Liz

JC:

Problems now is
not to go stark
screaming hysteric
cunt CENT pour cent 24
hours per day —
relapse after comfort &
Tuesday. = & mute MUTE —

olson saved my life.

St Elizabeth's Hospital, Washington DC. Pound's room, in the Chestnut Ward, is on the second floor, just above the car parked to the left of the central tower.

Pound's room, across the hall, 'was strewn with wadded papers, bits of envelopes, trampled books, pencils, lengths of string, cardboard files, trunks, old paint cans, jars filled with tea-bags or scraps of food. There was a dressing table with a huge mirror which reflected the glow of the sunset.'

Pound received many visitors, of course, during the long years of his confinement: indeed, he became the centre of something like a pilgrimage. His wife, Dorothy, was the most devoted. She lived in a cramped room near the hospital, and she came every day to visit her husband; she was to stay beside him until his eventual release. Dorothy Pound has been variously described as saintly, naive, cold – but her devotion, particularly after the emotional shocks which Pound had already forced her to endure, is remarkable.

Visitors came and went continually, despite the inevitable rifts and quarrels which marred all Pound's friendships. T. S. Eliot, e. e. cummings, Robert Lowell, William Carlos Williams, Conrad Aiken appeared and reappeared. After some time, Pound was allowed new privileges, and entertained his guests on the lawn of the hospital. His daughter remembers his 'tiny purse where he kept some coins for peanuts to feed the squirrels. "This is all I am allowed," he said, showing me the contents.' But, in a sense, he was happy. William Carlos Williams, in his *Autobiography*, recalls 'the same beard and restless twitching of the hands, shifting his shoulders about as he lay back in the chair studying me, the same bantering smile, screwing up his eyes, the half-coughing laugh and short, swift words, no sentence structure worth mentioning.' It was almost as if Pound were still a boy, with his enormous inchoate dreams, back in Pennsylvania.

But there were also more recent, and less agreeable, friends who sat with Pound. Fascists, racists and odd imponderables would come to pay willing homage to the poet who, they believed, was imprisoned by the government because of his beliefs. Pound's daughter described these people as 'sloppy and ignorant'. With them, she wrote, the atmosphere degenerated into one of 'vapid jokes' and boredom. And although Pound could still be witty and disarmingly candid in conversation about literary matters, in his political diatribes he was wilful, suspicious, and still virulently anti-Semitic.

The racist zealots and the acolytes were in a sense Pound's progeny. He liked his young visitors to call him 'Grampaw', in indirect homage to his own rumbustious and populist grandfather, Thaddeus; he still rambled on about politics and fidgeted incessantly while doing so, often greeting new callers with a lecture on Social Credit. Sometimes, however, he regained the high spirits of his past; when asked what he thought of Elvis Presley he replied, in his contrived folksy drawl, 'Waal, he's more entertaining than Frost or Sandburg.'

But his spirits were not always so robust; his competitive temperament was bruised by the rising reputations of his contemporaries: Frost himself but, more significantly, Eliot and Williams. He would become obsessive about the 'Hebes' and a Jewish conspiracy, and there were signs of incipient paranoia. Williams remembers him 'stating that he would be shot by an agent of the "International crew" the moment he stood outside the hospital gates.' And his multifarious correspondents were sworn to secrecy about the contents of his letters, even the fact that he was writing to them at all. 'God bloody Damn it and save one from one's friends,' he wrote to Louis Dudek in 1953. 'SHUT UP. You are NOT supposed to receive ANY letters from EP. They are UNSIGNED.'

Above all, there was the loneliness and weariness – the sense of things undone, 'the weariness of the man hit by history full blast', as his daughter had put it. The past was a treasured country, in a sense his only possession, which he was now in danger of losing: 'I can't hold two sides of an idea together but can live on memory if someone BRINGS it,' he wrote to Eileen Kinney, an old friend of Brancusi's. The present moment was now held only precariously by him. John Wain has written, 'He talked on and on in connected sentences and with perfect logic and persuasiveness; but if anyone interrupted him with a question it simply threw the needle out of the groove, and he fell silent for a moment, passed his hand wearily over his eyes, and then went on talking, starting from a different point.' Pound was aware of his predicament; he wrote to Archibald MacLeish in August 1955: 'I can't work here . . . The little and broken up time that I get (with no privacy and constant interruption and distraction) makes impossible that consecutive quality of feeling so important to me . . . this daily laceration and frustration of a creative impulse, carried on even a little while, can and surely will, with me I'm afraid, end with complete artistic impotence.' Some years later, in an interview with the *Paris Review*, Pound spoke of the struggle within his work 'to keep the value of a local and particular character, of a particular culture in this awful maelstrom, this awful avalanche toward uniformity. The whole fight is for the conservation of the individual soul.' This sense of life – and the threats under which it was forced to work – must in large part have been determined by his time at St Elizabeth's.

But, although he wrote to MacLeish of 'artistic impotence', he struggled hard and successfully to conserve himself. While in the hospital he worked continually on his poetry and his translations. Shortly after his release in 1958, he was to write to the superintendent of St Elizabeth's, Winfred Overholser, 'Dear W.O., I don't know whether you will ever get credit for making possible the Confucian Anthology and for two volumes of Cantos.' During this period, also, Pound's critical reputation began to rise after the long period of neglect or open hostility. He was awarded the Bollingen Prize for Poetry in 1949, for *Pisan Cantos*, and the subsequent uproar (in which the Library of Congress, who administered the prize, were accused of 'Fascist infiltration' and the jurors, who included Auden and Eliot, of condoning anti-Semitism) made that volume of poetry one of the most publicized of recent times. Pound's *Cantos*, up to and including the Pisan sequence, was published in 1948, and academic interest started to grow at a remarkable rate. Hugh Kenner published his pioneering *The Poetry of Ezra Pound* in 1951, and innumerable other critical studies have followed. Pound's selected letters were published in 1955 and, in the mid-Fifties, there was even *The Pound Newsletter*, devoted to his life and work.

Pound, of course, took a keen interest in all this activity – his correspondence was, as ever, voluminous, and he spread his advice, cautions and anger all over the world. He contributed to periodicals and helped intermittently to edit the *Square Dollar* series of publications. He became the centre of his own industry, an industry which even today shows no signs of diminishing. And yet he also managed, during this long period of busy confinement, to continue with his more significant work.

In 1954 Pound's translation of *The Classic Anthology* was published. He worked in his hospital room on this volume of odes, originally selected by Confucius, and the marks of his situation are there to be read:

> sorrow about the heart like an unwashed shirt, I
> clutch here at words,
> having no force to fly.

Pound had always exercised a significant force as a translator (his *Collected Translations* were published in 1953). He was, in both his life and his work, an extraordinarily skilful mimic whose most concise perceptions were often best carried through another person's voice.

But his own voice sometimes came through the camouflage and the muddle which surrounded him. In 1955, *Rock Drill* (Cantos 85–95) was published; it has been variously described as a 'mental diary' and a 'defensive manifesto'. It is in fact again concerned, at least in part, with monetary history and the course of Chinese civilization – a defiant restatement of Pound's central position – but in form and tone it goes beyond the scope of the preceding *Cantos*. Its purpose, according to Pound, is 'to move out from egoism and to establish some definition of an order possible or at any rate conceivable on earth.' The lines have been broken up, the writing is firm and elliptical but charged with meaning, as Pound deconstructs the conventional harmonies and rhythms of the verse unit. The obscurity in the sequence is of a different and more persuasive kind than that portentous variety which was offered in the *Pisan Cantos*; in *Rock Drill* it is the obscurity of the honed intellect moving from perception to perception until, together, they form a miraculous coherence:

> Love, gone as lightning,
>   enduring 5,000 years.
> Shall the comet cease moving
>   or the great stars be tied in one place!

In fact when *Rock Drill* is compared with the work of Pound's contemporaries – Williams, Eliot, and the others – the novelty of his enterprise becomes clear. Their work is more accessible, resting upon certain conventional truths of place and ideology; its perimeters are already known to the reader, and no further effort of comprehension is needed. Pound was moving outward, breaking open the language to reveal its potential richness. In so doing he broke open the world. He had always possessed a streak of rather coarse, but genuine, mysticism – and now, in his own work, he was beoming more and more attached to what he considered to be the permanent magical components of the universe. Such insights may be dismissed as lunatic or derivative, but it is significant that Pound's writing is at its most vibrant and powerful when it is animated by them:

> Lord, thaet scop the dayes lihte,
>   all that she knew was a spirit bright,
> A movement that moved in a cloth of gold
>   into her chamber.
> 'By the white dragon, under a stone
>   Merlin's fader is known to none.'

Rock Drill is the most persuasive sequence within the *Cantos*. *Thrones* (Cantos 96–109, published in 1959) continues with its exploration of the magical forces which are to be recaptured by the poet:

> lights blazed behind her
>   trees open, their minds stand before them . . .

but with a marked loss of power. The writing, especially in the passages of historical description, wavers slightly; there is a diminution of energy, only reprieved by passages of brilliant lyric and observation:

Form is cut in the lute's neck, tone is from the bowl.

This is, in fact, the enduring theme of the *Cantos*, whether Pound is describing the nature of money, good government or poetry itself. The struggle, as Pound perceived it, is toward particulars acutely perceived, toward an understanding of the actual, unclouded by vague generalities or the souped-up rhetoric of a stale language. In his early espousal of Imagism, just as much as in his attachment to Social Credit, Pound was always in pursuit of some simple and hard reality – a reality, in other words, which could be understood and manipulated.

But this interest in what is bright and tangible – the words freed from 'emotional slither' – was also a way of avoiding what lay beneath the surface. In Pound's case, this would undoubtedly include the mass of disturbed emotions which he never learned adequately to understand or to control. His own abandoned self was continually haunting him, pushing him from pose to pose until it becomes unclear where the mask ends and the man begins. In *The Women of Trachis*, a translation from Sophocles which Pound completed at St Elizabeth's, the hero appears in the 'mask of divine agony' which complemented Pound's own:

And now I'm in torture, no one to finish it off
with fire, or with a knife,
    or do ANYthing useful,
or even let me alone.

But one stage, at least, of Pound's personal ordeal was coming to an end. The pleas for his release from St Elizabeth's had begun in Europe in the mid-Fifties, and they were taken up by certain influential magazines – *Life* among them – in the United States. T. S. Eliot and Archibald MacLeish continued their public support and private enquiries for Pound; Robert Frost, America's poetic spokesman, agreed to intercede with the government. Dag Hammarskjold is said to have suggested Pound for the Nobel Prize for Literature in 1957; President Eisenhower himself was brought into the argument; a deal was done. The Attorney-General decided to drop all the charges against Pound, and the indictment for treason was dismissed on 18 April 1958. The *New York Times* reported, 'Mr Pound sat in the back of the court-room . . . His pockets were full of folded envelopes and other scraps of paper.' He had been in custody for thirteen years.

His new liberty released a kind of manic energy; he immediately visited Congressman Usher Burdick, who had played a large part in engineering his release. Pound was, as usual, voluble and nervous:

Opposite: Pound outside the federal courthouse, Washington, 18 April 1958, after the indictment of treason against him was dismissed. Dr Winfred Overholser, the Superintendent of St. Elizabeth's, swore in an affidavit that 'Ezra Pound is, and since December 4, 1945 has been, suffering from a paranoid state.' Pound was released into his wife's custody.

Dorothy and Ezra Pound at Fernbrook Avenue. When an old friend of the Pound family asked him if she might call him by his childhood nickname 'Ra', he replied: 'Well, I've been called worse things.'

Opposite: Brunnenburg Castle, Tirolo di Merano, Italy.

'This is an historic occasion . . . I am not anti-Semitic. I have been making jokes about Jews all my life . . . I might as well turn loose things you may not know . . . I must keep on the track. I'm talking too much. I don't have to tell it all in one day. I can come back . . . I've had the plug in for twelve years.' He was interviewed in these early days of his release by James Kilpatrick, the American columnist, who wrote, 'His restless hands are forever searching for glasses, or plucking pencil and notebook from breast pocket, or shaping ideas in the air. "No wonder my head hurts; all Europe fell on it; when I talk it is like an explosion in an art museum."' He spoke also of the *Cantos*: '"When you paint on a big canvas," he said, gesturing largely, "you have to start colours down here," gesturing small, "but it all ties in, it all ties in."'

Three days before sailing back to Europe, to which he had agreed to return, he visited Wyncote, Pennsylvania, the setting of his boyhood years. That night, he walked alone through the streets of the town – where he had once walked with Williams, discussing the future of poetry and the possibilities of his own life. On 30 June 1958, he boarded the *Cristoforo Colombo* with Dorothy Pound; at Naples he gave the Fascist salute to the photographers. It was as if he were returning to a world which had not changed since his confinement. When he landed in Genoa he seemed, for a while at least, to be back home. 'Who am I?' he said to bemused onlookers, 'I am famous. My name is in all the dictionaries . . . They used to say that my song was lively . . . They have never forgotten old Ez.'

On his arrival in Italy, he and Dorothy (together with a young American painter, Marcella Spann, who had visited Pound in St Elizabeth's in 1956) went to live with his daughter, Maria, and her husband in Brunnenburg Castle, near the village of Tirolo in the Italian Alps. This was to be the beginning of Pound's second incarceration, although in these last years it was to become a penitential form of self-imprisonment. At first everything went well. Pound's study was on the top floor of the castle's central tower. Gaudier's bust of the young Pound had been placed in the garden, where it caught the rays of the setting sun. The past was at last in its place, and the future looked promising. He wrote to friends that he felt good 'by conservative estimate, for twenty more years'. He went back to his hobby of carpentry and, when the BBC producer D. G. Bridson visited him, he talked clearly and cogently about his two central preoccupations: Confucius and economics. He gave an informal interview, in this first year, to a Swedish newspaper, *Dagens Nyheter*: 'If a small witty thing amuses him he'll burst out laughing loudly, or he'll wink maliciously.' Pound said in the same interview, 'I rest and I read, mostly historical works which are needed for my poetry, and just now I'm doing some proof-reading on Canto 98.' This Canto was part of the *Thrones* sequence, which was published in the following year. It was to be Pound's last major contribution to the *Cantos*.

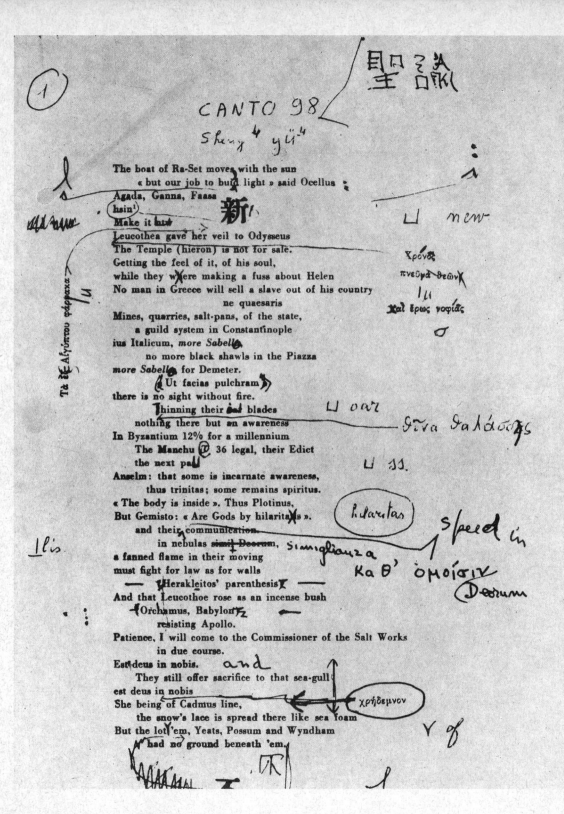

CANTO 98

The boat of Ra-Set moves with the sun
« but our job to build light » said Ocellus
Agada, Ganna, Faasa
hsin¹
Make it new
Leucothea gave her veil to Odysseus
The Temple (hieron) is not for sale.
Getting the feel of it, of his soul,
while they were making a fuss about Helen
No man in Greece will sell a slave out of his country
ne quaesaris
Mines, quarries, salt-pans, of the state,
a guild system in Constantinople
ius Italicum, *more Sabella*,
no more black shawls in the Piazza
more Sabella for Demeter.
« Ut facias pulchram »
there is no sight without fire.
Thinning their oat blades
nothing there but an awareness
In Byzantium 12% for a millennium
The Manchu @ 36 legal, their Edict
the next page
Anselm: that some is incarnate awareness,
thus trinitas; some remains spiritus.
« The body is inside ». Thus Plotinus,
But Gemisto: « Are Gods by hilaritas ».
and their communication
in nebulas simil Deorum,
a fanned flame in their moving
must fight for law as for walls
—— Herakleitos' parenthesis ——
And that Leucothoe rose as an incense bush
Orchamus, Babylon
resisting Apollo.
Patience, I will come to the Commissioner of the Salt Works
in due course.
Est deus in nobis.
They still offer sacrifice to that sea-gull
est deus in nobis
She being of Cadmus line,
the snow's lace is spread there like sea foam
But the lot 'em, Yeats, Possum and Wyndham
had no ground beneath 'em.

*Preceding page
Left:* Corrections to the text of
Canto XCVIII, part of the
Thrones sequence which Pound
completed on his return to Italy.
The 'Possum' mentioned in the
penultimate line is T. S. Eliot –
Pound was now reassessing his
old literary enthusiasms. *Above
right:* Dorothy Pound in the
garden of Brunnenburg Castle;
she is standing next to Gaudier-
Brzeska's bust of Pound, the
Hieratic Head. It was placed so as
to catch the rays of the setting
sun. *Below right:* Ezra and
Dorothy Pound at Brunnenburg,
c. 1960. They were not to spend
much more time together. 'If love
be not in the house there is
nothing,' (Canto CXVI).

By 1959, there were signs of the trouble to come. He was easily
fatigued – which, in a man of seventy-four, is perhaps not surprising –
but there were also indications of strain within the little family in the
castle. Maria, in *Discretions*, wrote, 'Something went wrong. The
house no longer contained a family. We were turning into entities who
should not have broken bread together . . . He was not happy . . . The
altitude oppressed him.' And so, as an escape, the Pounds (together
with Miss Spann) travelled to Rapallo. He was tired, anxious and,
Dorothy Pound wrote later, 'worried we would not have enough to
eat'. He sent a note to Ernest Hemingway in the October of that year:
'Old man him tired.' And in the same period he wrote, to Archibald
MacLeish, 'No use to myself or anyone . . . One thing to have Europe
fall on one's head. Another to be set in ruins of same.' At the end of
1959 Miss Spann, no doubt having had more than enough of the
Pounds' tribulations, returned to the United States. The Pounds went
back to Brunnenburg Castle.

But he couldn't stay in one place for long; in January 1960, he
travelled to Rome. Daniel Cory saw him there and wrote later in
Encounter that Pound 'was frankly embarrassed by his erratic and
nervous condition. As he said, "One day I talk like a parrot and the
next I can find nothing to say." ' Some days he was bouncy and alert,
striding through the streets of Rome in his baggy coat and bright
yellow scarf; on others, he was apathetic and despondent. All his
attempts to settle down had failed: 'It was obvious', Cory wrote, 'that
some profound emotional ebb tide was leaving him stranded and
incapable of any sustained concentration.' While in Rome, Pound
agreed to be interviewed by Donald Hall for the *Paris Review*; his talk
is full of doubts and misgivings:

If the individual, or heretic, gets hold of some essential truths, or sees some
error in the system being practised, he commits so many marginal errors
himself that he is worn out before he can establish his point . . . It is difficult to
write a paradise when all the superficial indications are that you ought to
write an apocalypse . . . Okay I am stuck . . . There is no doubt that the
writing is too obscure as it stands . . . Europe was a shock. The shock of no
longer feeling oneself in the center of something is probably part of it . . .
Somebody said that I am the last American living the tragedy of Europe.

By the summer of 1960 Pound was back in Brunnenburg Castle,
miserable and bitter. When Hilda Doolittle sent Pound the manuscript of her memoir of their friendship, *End to Torment*, he wrote back,
'Torment title excellent, but optimistic.' 'He was inconsolable . . .
living in the seclusion of his study,' Cory wrote. His health had
deteriorated, and he went into a clinic. Dorothy Pound wrote to
Harry Meacham, a family friend who had played a large part in
Pound's release from St Elizabeth's, 'Ezra seems oppressed always by
some sense of not having done what he should with his life . . . Too
much terrible anxiety loaded onto such a sensitivity.' Pound himself
wrote to Meacham, 'The plain fact is that my head just doesn't
WORK. Stretches when it just doesn't work.'

At the beginning of 1961, however, he was back in Rome again for a brief revival; he was surrounded by acolytes – 'campy', one observer described them – and was photographed at the head of a neo-Fascist parade. But this grotesque 'social' life proved too strenuous; his health broke down again and he was brought back, sick, to the clinic near Brunnenburg. A friend of Pound's daughter, Perdita Schaffner, recalls, 'Mary had warned me that her father was very depressed. She explained the nature and course of his illness; the euphoria of the homecoming followed by reaction – frustration, rages, dejection, unpredictable moods.' Pound was very ill (a compound of extreme fatigue, inability to eat, and prostate complications), and he needed constant attention; his wife, in her own words, 'could no longer cope with the situation.'

At this point Maria evidently wrote to her mother, Olga Rudge, to ask for help. During this period, and during the time when Pound was in St Elizabeth's, Miss Rudge was in an unenviable position, denied access to the man whom she still loved and venerated. According to her daughter, she felt 'hurt and humiliated from all sides'. During Pound's long absence she had kept 'everything. Embalmed.' But in Pound's illness she came; she was efficient and practical; she could look after Pound in ways that Dorothy could not; she took him back with her to Sant'Ambrogio. They were to commute between here and Venice for the rest of Pound's life.

It was at the end of 1961 that Pound turned to silence. 'I did not enter silence. Silence captured me,' he was to say later (*Time*, 15 November 1965). The condition has been described as one of schizophrenic depression, with its origins in Pound's experience of the cage at Pisa; it has been seen merely as a symptom of his utter despondency; it has even been described as another gesture, a masquerade, the final camouflage behind which he could remain inviolable. Whatever its origins, it was sustained by Pound to the end, with little interruption. He spent much of his time sitting, staring into space, brooding. He now relied entirely upon Olga Rudge: she shopped, she cleaned, she looked after his medication. She was a nurse, a mother and a disciple. His long silences were legendary and awesome. His conversation, when it came, as Richard Stern remembers it in *Paideuma*, was fragmentary: '"How are you, Mr Pound?" "Senile . . . Wrong, wrong, wrong. I've always been wrong. You don't know what it's like to get off on the wrong path . . . Not to remember."' He was also expressing more and more severe reservations about the nature of his work; to the critic, Michael Alexander, he said, 'I have lots of fragments. I can't make much sense of them, and I don't suppose anyone else will.'

The Italian magazine, *Epoca*, came to interview Pound in 1963. He gave the impression of 'a vanquished man, sad eyes, tired voice, the phrases come slowly, immobile limbs'. The restlessness, the energy, and all the early self-confidence had vanished: 'Too late came the understanding,' Pound is quoted as saying, 'too late came the uncertainty of knowing nothing . . . Everything is so difficult, so

useless . . . I no longer work, I do nothing.' His work on the *Cantos* had now come to a virtual halt. Daniel Cory records a conversation he had with him about his poetry at this time: '"It's a botch," he said firmly. "I knew too little about so many things . . . I picked out this and that thing that interested me, and then jumbled them into a bag. But that's not the way to make," – and he paused for a moment – "a *work* of art."' But the last drafts and fragments of the *Cantos*, which he had been working on since his return to Italy and until his silence, tend to disprove that lachrymose reassessment. The lines have the lightness of total, disciplined attention – the stray phrases and harmonies breaking through into vision. It is almost as if the whole previous stretch of the *Cantos* was a preparation for these moments of power, when the dross is stripped away and a pure language reveals itself:

> A blown husk that is finished
> but the light sings eternal
> a pale flare over marshes.

Above and overleaf: Pound in Venice, 1963 – two years after Pound had withdrawn into silence. He had now returned to that place where he had first emerged as a poet. 'I have blundered always,' he said in an interview.

Opposite: Pound in an art gallery in Venice, *c.* 1967; behind him, a bronze image of himself.

Pound with Stephen Spender, the English poet, at the Spoleto Festival in 1969.

In 1965 Pound and Olga Rudge travelled to the Spoleto Festival, where Pound's opera, *Le Testament*, was performed as a ballet. Charles Olson saw him here and wrote, 'It was very beautiful the way the fierceness of Pound had settled down into a voiceless thing.' Then Pound and Rudge travelled to Paris, where he refused to look at the French Academy when it was pointed out to him – a theatrical but telling gesture. In the autumn of that year they travelled to Greece where, according to Michael Reck (in *Ezra Pound: a Close-Up*), he 'saw the Castalian springs, and drank of them.'

During this last decade of his life, he was in and out of clinics – 'continually searching for the cure', as C. David Heymann has written in *The Last Rower*, 'which would restore his creative faculties'; in Montreux, he was even injected with the cells of sheep. During this period, also, Pound became finally and irrevocably estranged from his wife, who had stood by him so patiently for so many years. Dorothy now spent half the year in Rapallo, half the year in England. When they were both in Rapallo, Olga and Dorothy themselves never met or alluded to each other; there was – and continues to be – a profound silence about the nature of their respective lives. In December 1970, Dorothy Pound wrote to Harry Meacham, 'I do not know where E.P. is . . . I have not seen him in eighteen months.' Between 1969 and 1972, she met him only twice; they were in the same row at a concert in Rapallo, but Pound ignored her.

In the late Sixties, Pound began a series of visits in order to repossess a little of his past. 'Cocteau called me the rower on the river of the dead,' he said in an interview, '"le rameur sur le fleuve des morts"; it is sad to look back.' This was in 1968; he had already travelled to Zurich, the year before, to see the grave of James Joyce.

Opposite: Pound reading at the Spoleto Festival, 1969.

Overleaf
Pound at the grave of James Joyce in Zurich, 1967. 'Joyce's name with Nora's sat in a corner of the cemetery,' he said later, 'the names nearly illegible on a stone hidden in the grass.'

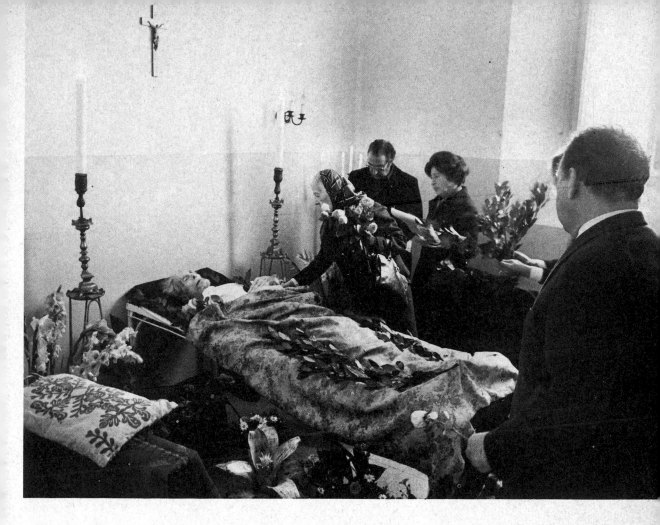

In 1965, he had gone to London for the memorial service for T. S. Eliot, and had flown on to Ireland to visit the widow of W. B. Yeats. And then, in 1969, he travelled back to the United States for the last time; he saw the manuscript of *The Waste Land*, recently rediscovered, in the New York Public Library. Everything else had gone now. He had outlived everyone – Gaudier-Brzeska, Hemingway, Lewis, Eliot, Joyce, Cocteau, Yeats, William Carlos Williams. He was the last of a generation which had tried to create art and literature on an heroic scale.

Pound had once said to Robert Lowell of his own destiny, 'To begin with a swelled head and end with swelled feet.' Pound had always been invaded by such contradictions, and was sometimes impaled upon them. The insecurity and brittleness of his temperament, however, had become a divining rod of the age's character – reflecting its darkest sides as well as its brighter, more heroically individual, aspects. It was also this mangled and difficult identity which gave his poetry its powerful and complex shape. Pound lived during a period when there was no significant context for his intuitions and his

Olga Rudge, beside the body of Pound, 2 November 1972.

Opposite: One of the last photographs of Pound, in his working room in Venice, 1971.

*M'amour, m'amour
    what do I love and
        where are you?*

*That I lost my center
        fighting the world.*

*The dreams clash
        and are shattered –
and that I tried to make a paradiso
                        terrestre.*

115

sometimes wayward perceptions; and so he set out, single-handed, to create one. The *Cantos* were to reconstruct a whole order – historical, natural, cultural – but it was an impossible job. Pound had written, in 1928, of 'a man hurling himself at an indomitable chaos, and yanking and hauling as much of it as possible into some sort of order (or beauty)', and this was to be Pound's own role for the next forty years. When the *Cantos* work, when it all coheres, it is a stupendous affirmation of the imagination and of the visionary powers of poetry; when it fails, or falls into obscurity, it is at least the heroic measure of what one man set out to achieve. Pound attempted to recreate the whole world in the image of himself and his poetry – despite the divisive tendencies of the age, and the obsessive weaknesses of his own character. He adhered to a visionary view of the world that the world itself could hardly understand. Ezra Pound died on 1 November 1972 in Venice; Dorothy Pound died in the following year.

A tail-piece designed by Dorothy Shakespear for the *Cantos*.

1885 30 October: Ezra Loomis Pound born in Hailey, Idaho, the only child of Homer and Isabel Pound

1901 Pound is enrolled at the University of Pennsylvania, Philadelphia, where he meets William Carlos Williams

1903 Enrolled at Hamilton College, near Utica in New York State

1906 Harrison Fellow in Romanics at the University of Pennsylvania. Travels to Europe (his third visit) to research into the work of Lope de Vega and Provençal poets. He finds here the imaginative terrain of his life

1907 Employed as instructor in Romance Languages at Wabash College, Crawfordsville, Indiana

1908 Pound's academic career ends with his being expelled from Wabash College for a minor sexual indiscretion, and he travels to Gibraltar and Venice. *A Lume Spento* published in Italy. The self-conscious *poète maudit* is born, and towards the end of the year he moves to London

1909–13 Based in London, but frequently visits Europe; works hard to promote his literary career both as a poet and critic. Associates with W. B. Yeats, Ford Madox Ford, Wyndham Lewis and James Joyce. Founds Imagism. He also meets the sculptor, Henri Gaudier-Brzeska, and becomes involved in extra-literary propagandizing. *Exultations, Personae, Canzoni* and *Ripostes* published

1914 April: Marries Dorothy Shakespear. Meets and enthusiastically promotes T. S. Eliot; becomes involved with Vorticism and *Blast*

1915–18 Acts as unpaid literary agent for Lewis, Joyce and Eliot. Increasingly dissatisfied with the London literary establishment; meets Major C. H. Douglas, whose doctrines of Social Credit confirm Pound's disgust at metropolitan commercialism. *Cathay, Lustra* and *Homage to Sextus Propertius* published; the first *Three Cantos* and the *Hell Cantos* written

1920 Travels to Paris, Provence and Sirmione, where meets James Joyce for the first time. *Hugh Selwyn Mauberley* published

1921–22 The Pounds move to Paris. Pound enjoys the company of Cocteau and Picabia and of musicians, among them Ravel, Stravinsky and Copland. He works on his opera *Le Testament*. Through Tristan Tzara and Louis Aragon is involved in Dadaism. Of the Americans in

Paris he associates with e. e. cummings, Ernest Hemingway and Olga Rudge. Resumes work on the *Cantos*. Edits the rough manuscripts of Eliot's *The Waste Land*

1923 Meets George Antheil and Gertrude Stein briefly. Finishes revising the first sixteen cantos

1924 Having grown tired of Paris, the Pounds move on to Rapallo in Italy; Olga Rudge follows. Pound now begins extensive work on new cantos

1925 Olga Rudge gives birth to a daughter, Maria

1926 Dorothy Pound gives birth to a son, Omar. *Le Testament* is performed in Paris. *A Draft of XVI Cantos* published in Paris

1930–39 During this period in Italy, Pound continues with his work on the *Cantos* (*A Draft of XXX Cantos*, *Eleven New Cantos* and *The Fifth Decad of Cantos* published) and at the same time publishes a succession of prose works, both economic and literary: *Make it New*, *Guide to Kulchur*, *ABC of Reading*, *ABC of Economics*, *Social Credit: an Impact*. He organizes a series of concerts in Rapallo. His political activities become more pronounced and obsessive. Meets Mussolini in 1933

1939 Visits America, ostensibly to prevent its involvement in the War. Alienates all of his friends

1940 His journalism and his, by now voluminous, correspondence is devoted to the support of Mussolini and Hitler

1941 Application to return to the United States turned down. Begins his broadcasts, against the Allies, for Rome Radio

1943 Indicted for treason by the American Attorney-General

1945 April: Arrested by partisans, and delivered to the American military authorities. Taken to Pisa detention camp in May. Writes *Pisan Cantos*. In November flown to Washington and imprisoned in Washington jail. 27 November found unfit to stand trial. 21 December transferred to St Elizabeth's Hospital for the insane

1949 Pound awarded the Bollingen Prize for *Pisan Cantos*, thereby provoking a political and literary storm

1950–54 Critical interest in Pound revives and, while confined in St Elizabeth's, he becomes the active centre of his own literary industry. 'Pilgrims' come to listen to him but, despite this, he manages to work consistently on his poetry and his translations (*Rock Drill*, *Collected Translations*, *The Classic Anthology*) and maintains his undiminished correspondence

1955–56 The campaign for his release gathers momentum, in both the United States and Europe

1958 18 April: Pound's indictment for treason is dismissed, and he returns to Italy with Dorothy. They live with his daughter, Maria

1959–61 Pound is querulous and ill, unable to settle in his new life, visits Rapallo and Rome, and is disillusioned with both his work and his previous career. *Thrones* published. 1961: Olga Rudge returns to him, and takes charge. His silence descends

1965 Pound travels to London, to the memorial service for Eliot, to Ireland to visit Yeats's widow, to Spoleto to see *Le Testament* performed as a ballet, and to Greece

1967   Visits Paris, by now a hero, and Zurich to see Joyce's grave

1969   Visits New York, where he sees the newly discovered manuscript of Eliot's *The Waste Land*. Everyone and everything else gone.

1972   1 November: Pound dies in Venice.

1973   8 December: Dorothy Pound dies near Cambridge, England

BIBLIOGRAPHY

GENERAL

Michael Alexander: *The Poetic Achievement of Ezra Pound* London 1979

Christine Brooke-Rose: *A ZBC of Ezra Pound* London 1971

William Cookson: *A Guide to the Cantos of Ezra Pound* London 1985.

Donald Davie: *Pound* London 1975

Hugh Kenner: *The Poetry of Ezra Pound* London 1951

Hugh Kenner: *The Pound Era* London 1972

FURTHER READING

Agenda: Ezra Pound Issue October–November, 1965

Conrad Aiken: *Ushant* New York 1952

Richard Aldington: *Life for Life's Sake* New York 1941

Alice Steiner Amdur: *The Poetry of Ezra Pound* Cambridge, Mass. 1936

George Antheil: *Bad Boy of Music* London 1947

Massimo Bacigalupo: *The Formed Trace: The Later Poetry of Ezra Pound* New York 1980

Sylvia Beach: *Shakespeare and Company* London 1960

Ian Bell: *Critic as Scientist: The Modernist Poetics of Ezra Pound* London 1981

Ronald Bush: *The Genesis of Ezra Pound's Cantos* Princeton 1976

William M. Chace: *The Political Identities of Ezra Pound and T. S. Eliot* Stanford 1973

Julien Cornell: *The Trial of Ezra Pound* New York 1966

John Cournos: *Autobiography* New York 1935

Malcolm Cowley: *Exile's Return* New York 1934

H. D. (Hilda Doolittle): *An End to Torment: A Memoir of Ezra Pound* New York 1979

Reed Way Dasenbrock: *The Literary Vorticism of Ezra Pound and Wyndham Lewis: Towards the Condition of Painting* Baltimore 1985

Donald Davie: *Ezra Pound. Poet as Sculptor* London 1965

Earle Davis: *Vision Fugitive. Ezra Pound and Economics* Kansas 1968

George Dekker: *Sailing After Knowledge. The Cantos of Ezra Pound* London 1963

L. S. Dembo: *The Confucian Odes of Ezra Pound* London 1963

N. Christoph De Nagy: *The Poetry of Ezra Pound. The Pre-Imagist Stage* Berne 1968

T. S. Eliot: *The Waste Land. A Facsimile and Transcript of the Original Drafts, edited by V. Eliot* London 1971

Richard Ellman: *Eminent Domain* New York 1967

John J. Espey: *Ezra Pound's Mauberley* London 1955

John Gould Fletcher: *Life is My Song* New York 1937

Wendy Flory: *Ezra Pound and His Cantos* New Haven 1984

Ford Madox Ford: *Return to Yesterday* London 1931

Ford Madox Ford: *Thus to Revisit* London 1921

G. S. Fraser: *Ezra Pound* London 1960

Christine Froula: *To Write Paradise: Style and Error in Pound's Cantos* New Haven 1984

Donald Gallup: *A Bibliography of Ezra Pound* London 1963

Donald Gallup: *T. S. Eliot and Ezra Pound* New Haven 1970

K. L. Goodwin: *The Influence of Ezra Pound* London 1966

Donald Hall: *Remembering Poets* New York 1978

Eva Hesse (editor): *New Approaches to Ezra Pound* London 1969

C. David Heymann: *Ezra Pound. The Last Rower* London 1976

Alan Holder: *Three Voyagers in Search of Europe* Philadelphia 1966

Eric Homberger: *Ezra Pound. The Critical Heritage* London 1972

Patricia Hutchins: *Ezra Pound's Kensington* London 1965

Thomas H. Jackson: *The Early Poetry of Ezra Pound* Cambridge, Mass. 1968

Alfred Kreymbourg: *Troubadour* New York 1925

Jeanette Lander: *Ezra Pound* New York 1971

James Laughlin: *Gists and Piths: A Memoir of Ezra Pound* Iowa 1982

Lewis Leary (editor): *Motive and Method in the Cantos of Ezra Pound* New York 1954

Wyndham Lewis: *Blasting and Bombardiering* London 1937

Wyndham Lewis: *Time and Western Man* London 1927

Brita Lindberg-Seyersted (editor): *Pound/Ford: The Story of a Literary Friendship* London 1982

Robert McAlmon and Kay Boyle: *Being Geniuses Together* London 1970

Peter Makin: *Pound's Cantos* London 1985

Timothy Materer (editor): *Pound/Lewis. The Letters of Ezra Pound and Wyndham Lewis* London 1985

Harry M. Meacham: *The Caged Panther. Ezra Pound at St. Elizabeth's* New York 1967

Eustace Mullins: *This Difficult Individual, Ezra Pound* New York 1961

E. P. Nassar: *The Cantos of Ezra Pound* Baltimore 1975

Charles Norman: *The Case of Ezra Pound* New York 1948

Charles Norman: *Ezra Pound* New York 1960

William O'Connor and Edward Stone (editors): *A Casebook on Ezra Pound* New York 1959

Paideuma: A Journal Devoted to Ezra Pound Scholarship. University of Maine

D. D. Paige (editor): *The Selected Letters of Ezra Pound, 1907–1941* London 1950

Paris Review. No 28 (1962). 'Interview with Ezra Pound'

Daniel Pearlman: *The Barb of Time. On the Unity of Ezra Pound's Cantos* New York 1969

Dorothy Pound: *Etruscan Gate* Exeter 1971

Ezra Pound Newsletter Berkeley, California 1954–56

Omar Pound and A. Walton Litz (editors): *Ezra Pound and Dorothy Shakespear: Their Letters, 1910–1914* London 1985

Bernetta Quinn: *Ezra Pound* New York 1972

Jean-Michel Rabaté: *Language, Sexuality and Ideology in Ezra Pound's Cantos* London 1986

Mary de Rachewiltz: *Discretions* London 1971

Forrest Read (editor): *Pound/Joyce* London 1968

Michael Reck: *Ezra Pound. A Close-Up* London 1967

J. A. Robbins (editor): *EP to LU* Bloomington 1963

Peter Russell (editor): *Ezra Pound* London 1950

R. Murray Schafer (editor): *Ezra Pound and Music* London 1978

Catherine Seelye (editor): *Charles Olson & Ezra Pound. An Encounter at St Elizabeth's* New York 1975

Paul Smith: *Pound Revised* London 1983

Noel Stock: *The Life of Ezra Pound* London 1970

Noel Stock: *Poet in Exile* Manchester 1964

Noel Stock: *Reading the Cantos* London 1967

J. P. Sullivan: *Ezra Pound* London 1970

J. P. Sullivan: *Ezra Pound and Sextus Propertius* London 1965

Leon Surette: *A Light from Eleusis: A Study of Ezra Pound's Cantos* Oxford 1979

Walter Sutton (editor): *Ezra Pound. A Collection of Critical Essays* Englewood Cliffs 1963

Carroll F. Terrell: *A Companion to the Cantos of Ezra Pound* Berkeley, California 1980

E. Fuller Torrey: *The Roots of Treason: Ezra Pound and St Elizabeth's* London 1984

Harold W. Watts: *Ezra Pound and the Cantos* London 1952

William Carlos Williams: *Autobiography* London 1968

Hugh Witemeyer: *The Poetry of Ezra Pound, 1908–1920* Berkeley, California 1969

Anthony Woodward: *Ezra Pound and the Pisan Cantos* London 1980

George T. Wright: *The Poet in the Poem* Berkeley, California 1960

W. B. Yeats: *A Packet for Ezra Pound* Dublin 1929

WORKS BY EZRA POUND

POETRY

A Lume Spento Venice 1908
A Quinzaine for this Yule London 1908
Personae London 1909
Exultations London 1909
Provença Boston 1910
Canzoni London 1911
The Sonnets and Ballate of Guido Cavalcanti London 1912
Ripostes London 1912
Cathay London 1915
Lustra London 1916
Quia Pauper Amavi London 1919
Hugh Selwyn Mauberley London 1920
Umbra London 1920
Poems 1918–1921 New York 1921
A Draft of XVI Cantos Paris 1925
Personae: The Collected Poems of Ezra Pound New York 1926
Selected Poems, edited by T. S. Eliot London 1928
A Draft of XXX Cantos Paris 1930
Eleven New Cantos New York 1934
Homage to Sextus Propertius London 1934
Cantos LII–LXXI New York 1934
The Fifth Decad of Cantos London 1937
Pisan Cantos New York 1948
The Translations of Ezra Pound London 1953
The Classic Anthology defined by Confucius Cambridge, Mass. 1954
Section: Rock Drill: 85–95 de los cantares Milan 1955
Sophocles: The Women of Trachis. A Version by Ezra Pound London 1956
Thrones: 96–109 de los cantares Milan 1959
The Cantos of Ezra Pound London 1964
Selected Cantos London 1967
Late Cantos and Fragments New York 1969
The Cantos London 1975
Selected Poems, 1908–1959 London 1975
Collected Early Poems New York 1976

PROSE

The Spirit of Romance London 1910
Gaudier-Brzeska. A Memoir London 1916
Pavannes and Divisions New York 1918
Instigations New York 1920
Antheil and the Treatise on Harmony Paris 1924
ABC of Economics London 1933
ABC of Reading London 1934
Make It New London 1934
Jefferson and/or Mussolini London 1935
Polite Essays London 1937
Guide To Kulchur London 1938
If This Be Treason Siena 1948
Patria Mia Chicago 1950
Literary Essays of Ezra Pound London 1954
Pavannes and Divagations Norfolk, Connecticut 1958
Impact: Essays on Ignorance and the Decline of American Civilisation Chicago 1960
Confucius: The Great Digest, The Unwobbling Pivot, The Analects New York 1969
Selected Prose London 1973
Certain Radio Speeches of Ezra Pound Rotterdam 1975

ANTHOLOGIES

Des Imagistes London 1914
Catholic Anthology London 1915
Active Anthology London 1933
Confucius to Cummings: An Anthology of Poetry New York 1964

LIST OF ILLUSTRATIONS

INDEX

A figure 2 in brackets immediately after a page number indicates that there are two separate references on that page. Page numbers in *italics* refer to illustrations. E. P. stands for Ezra Pound.